MAN 1, BANK 0.

A TRUE STORY OF LUCK, DANGER, DILEMMA AND ONE MAN'S EPIC, $95,000 BATTLE WITH HIS BANK.

BY PATRICK COMBS

ISBN: 1453632301

ISBN-13: 9781453632307

LCCN: 2010908814

This is an entirely true story. I took copious notes while it was going on to protect myself. I dedicate it to anyone who has felt pushed around or screwed by a large corporation. And I dedicate it to all who have stood up for themselves based on principle. Fight the good fight.

TABLE OF CONTENTS

You May Already Be a Winner

Ralph Waldo Emerson boldly stated, "Don't be too timid and squeamish about your actions. All life is an experiment." In May of 1995, I suddenly found myself smack in the middle of a very unusual "life experiment." I deposited a phony check into my ATM as a joke. It came as junk mail, pushing a get-rich-quick scheme. To my absolute astonishment, it cashed. Thus began the wildest adventure I've ever been on in my life.

ACCOUNT HISTORY

At the beginning of May 1995, I imagine 99 percent of First Interstate Bank employees viewed their bank as a company built to last and only getting better. They had so much going for them. The slogan on their stationary proudly declared, "We Mean Business," and they did. They were now firmly established as the tenth largest bank in the nation, with eleven hundred branches spread out mostly in the western United States. They kept finding new ways to compete in a competitive marketplace where offers for free checking were suddenly commonplace. Their most recent innovation was the "$5 Perfect Service Guarantee." If they made a mistake and you, the customer, called it to their attention, they would give you $5 in cold hard cash, right there on the spot. First Interstate was the only bank confident enough to offer such a thing.

Speaking of confidence, I also imagine that in some corner window office on some high floor of the First Interstate Tower, the second tallest building in Los Angeles, perhaps just below the top floor—on the sixty-first floor—some executive was still very actively monitoring and tracking the return on investment of the bank's expanding network of automated teller machines. ATMs were still relatively new to most of us. Yes, they first went into use in 1972 in the United Kingdom, but in 1995 in the United States, their ready availability on every street corner couldn't have been more than four years old. Using the outside ATM rather than going into the bank and waiting in a teller's line was still something you noticed as a new feature.

The executive I imagine running the numbers was surely smiling at the way ATMs were increasing the bank's profits by eliminating the need for tellers and giving the bank a reason to charge a $1 service fee on every ATM cash withdrawal.

Perhaps he pictured to himself that all those dollars would stack up higher than the skyscraper he was sitting in. The very same skyscraper that had caught fire seven years prior on the twelfth floor just after 10:00 p.m., burning for four hours, destroying five floors, injuring forty people, and leaving one maintenance worker dead when the elevator the worker was riding opened onto the burning twelfth floor.

It was the worst high-rise fire in the history of Los Angeles, requiring the combined efforts of sixty-four fire companies, ten city rescue ambulances, seventeen private ambulances, four helicopters, fifty-three command officers and support personnel, a complement of 383 firefighters and paramedics, and considerable assistance from other city guardians.

The fire got completely out of control because the building was not equipped with a sprinkler system, which was not required for office towers at the time of construction in 1973. The fire was eventually contained at 2:19 a.m., but had caused $50 million in damages. These were dark days for First Interstate. The bank posted losses in the hundreds of millions for 1987, 1989, and 1991, mostly because of bad real estate loans and the severe recession in California.

Rumors of a takeover were rife in the early 1990s, but that was all behind First Interstate now, because in 1995, under the stewardship of Chief Executive Officer Bill Siart, First Interstate was on fire in a new sense of the word.

Two thousand miles away, somewhere in Columbus, Ohio, I imagine that Mitch Klass was feeling really good, too. He was not a CEO of a Fortune 500, but he was captain of his own financial empire. Perhaps on the same day that an executive on the sixty-first floor of a bank tower in Los Angeles was smiling out the window, Mitch Klass was at a local print shop smiling at the results. Because, like the bank, he too had found a way to basically "print money," as they say.

As long as the print offer was financially sexy enough, the money would come pouring into his post office box. Mitch was good with words, old school. He could write copy that sold. Using the same twenty-six letters available to everyone else who knew English, and a truckload of exclamation points, Mitch Klass could entice thousands to buy on the promise of getting rich quick.

But this time, he was taking it to a whole new level; words and numbers in the configuration of a seemingly real $95,000 bank check!! Perhaps he smelled the ink across the fake-enticing check and admired his wordcraft just below it on the attached letter: "We took in this amount in just 3 weeks!!" Perhaps he marveled at the printer's ability to customize each of the millions of checks with individual names and addresses. Perhaps he dropped the first completely stuffed, ready-to-go envelope ceremoniously into a mailbox and wished it luck before climbing into what I imagine to be a Mercedes. Mitch Klass was about to get rich quick, again.

Meanwhile, in San Francisco, I know exactly what was going on with me. But rather than tell you straight out, I prefer to imagine a scenario that I believe may have taken place further into this story. It's highly likely an investigator of some sort was employed to find out all that he could about me, perhaps with the words, "I want to know everything we can know about this guy. What he does for a living, if he has a criminal record, outstanding parking tickets, how much he has in his bank accounts, any other bank accounts he holds, what family he has and where they live, and how much money they have. Where he lives and what time he leaves his home in the morning and what time he gets back and where he stops to eat or get his kicks along the way. I want to know everything about this punk by tomorrow!"

And I like to imagine that the investigator did a great job and returned the next day with a full and detailed report, revealing that I lived in the Cole Valley neighborhood of San Francisco at 326 Carl Street, an apartment I was renting. That I worked for myself as a motivational speaker talking to college students about how to succeed. That I apparently wasn't very good at it, as I had $45,000 of credit card debt spread out across five different credit cards, and only one other account, a savings account of $71. That I'd just had my first book published, a book for students titled *Major in Success*, which had yet to pay me a dime in royalties. I drove an old 1977 Burgundy Ford Granada that I'd purchased on the cheap for $1,500.

I was twenty-nine years of age, born and raised in Bend, Oregon. A year of college at Lewis and Clark College in Portland, Oregon. And then four more years and a bachelor's degree in speech and communications from San Francisco State University, where I made ends meet with student loans and jobs as a janitor and at the campus day-care center. That after college I'd messed around managing rock bands and worked for Levi Strauss and Company for a year before quitting to go into speaking. That I had family; a mother in Portland, also with no savings, and a married older brother in Boston, making it, but not wealthy.

I'd gotten married at twenty-six years old but was recently separated and filing divorce papers. I did in fact have unpaid parking tickets, and a criminal record. As a teenager I was brought to a police station for breaking the letter *C* off the lighted sign attached to the outside wall of the local mall that said "Cinema," for the stated reason of "wanting to see if I could climb up onto it." No charges were filed, but community service was required, as well as $1,500 in damages.

Additionally, I had a warrant issued for my arrest at twenty-two years old for ignoring a $50 fine I'd received for riding the Muni train without a proper ticket. I'd been picked up for that warrant when found in a hot tub that I did not have permission to use on the private property of a condominium village. I'd spent the night in jail and was released in the morning with the satisfaction of the debt. And on a third illegal note, my driver's license was suspended for an unpaid bill from the insurance company that covered the parked car I'd gingerly backed into, causing a dime-sized dent in the bumper and incurring an outsized $1,500 repair claim.

As an uninsured driver, the $1,500 was my obligation. As a person who'd walked door to door through the rain that night to notify the car's owner that I'd put a small dent in his bumper and wanted to pay for the damage, I was refusing to pay the bill because it was grossly disproportionate to the amount of damage I'd done and no one consulted me on who to get a repair bid from. So when the DMV gave me the option to "pay this debt or lose your license for a year," I gladly switched from driving to busing.

And when the DMV repeated itself a year later, I kept on busing it. And when the DMV repeated itself a year later, still my car continued to accumulate no mileage. The DMV regulations state that after seven years, they'd have to give me back my license no matter what, but it was unclear whether I would hold out that long. Other than that, apparently twenty-nine years of lawful living. And, finally, the investigator would have found out that I'd been with First Interstate bank as a "customer in good standing" for twelve years. As a matter of fact, First Interstate was the only bank I'd ever used in my life.

And then I like to imagine that the investigator paused, perhaps first looking out the skyscraper window, and then said, "One other thing. And it may be meaningless. But every driver's license photo this guy has ever taken is apparently a joke. In every photo he seems to make a deliberate attempt to make himself look different or odd or funny in his photo. Nerd. Hippy. Criminal. Like I said, it could just be meaningless, but I thought I should tell you. Plus, in his high school year book, he's voted 'Class Clown.' "

PRESENT BALANCE

As I step up to use the outdoor ATM, there's a blond-haired young man wearing a knitted Rastafarian hat panhandling for change. His cardboard sign makes me laugh: *"If you lived HERE you'd be homeless by now."* I give him a dollar in change. He's a regular by First Interstate's Haight-Ashbury branch.

After fifteen minutes waiting in line for the ATM, it's finally my turn. As I step up to get some cash, a little window on the panel slides from green to red. It now says "closed."

What? No. This is not perfect service, I think to myself.

I glance over at the other ATM working to my left. To use it I would have to cut into the line, or start over again on the wait. This is not *perfect* service. This is a *mistake*. I round the corner and walk up First Interstate's dirty steps.

I get the cute red-headed teller. She's friendly.

"Hi, how may I help you?"

"Hi. Uhm, listen. I waited in line for the ATM, and then right when it was my turn, it closed," I say.

"Oh, I'm sorry about that. It's being refreshed."

"Well, might I have $5 for the inconvenience of having to come in the bank—you know—because of the $5 Perfect Service Guarantee?"

A man $45,000 in debt cannot be blamed for asking.

"Well, you're still able to do your banking, sir. I *can* help you."

"I know, but the wasted time in line and having to come into the bank—definitely not *perfect* service. Know what I mean?"

She's smiling. She thinks it's funny.

"Oh ...okay, sir. I see what you're saying. Here's your $5."

And with that, she hands me a crisp five-spot.

I will marry this teller, grow old with this bank, and always hunt for ATMs that are closed.

I ask her for my bank balance, which, as I struggle to make ends meet, consistently bounces between a couple of thousand in the black and several thousand in the red.

"Twelve years with the bank, Mr. Combs. You must have opened your account when you were nine."

Flirting with me. I didn't see that coming.

"Actually I was sixteen—At nine I was amassing my great fortune."

"I understand. Here's your balance, Mr. Combs," she says, smiling while sliding me a slip of paper that says on it, "$43.12"

"My other account is offshore."

"I understand. Have a good day, Mr. Combs."

Shit, and with $7,000 worth of bills sitting on my desk and only three checks coming in the next three months of summer, I'm going to have to open another credit card.

$95,093.35 ENCLOSED

On the way into my home, I grab the mail from the black mailbox that hangs on the iron gate that encloses the stairs. One is a check for $2,250 from a college where I did one of my motivational speeches. Another is also a check from a college, this one for $1,750. This is a banner day! But, alas, three more bills are in the stack. Two from credit card companies—each carrying a minimum balance due of more than $300.

And then I see it. In the stack of mail there is a gray envelope with a small cellophane window which displays a check inside made out to my name. On the envelope it says, *"95,093.35 enclosed."*

I don't believe it for a second, but nonetheless I will take the bait and open it. I will relish the opportunity to see a check for all that money made out to my name, even if it's not real. A man must have dreams. And a man must look *just in case* he *actually* won something. Perhaps a contest that he'd forgotten he entered. Perhaps a random drawing that has made him rich overnight. So you open the envelope to look, and to dream even if for just a brief moment. But you tear the envelope knowing there is no real hope. Knowing Ed McMahon loves the tease.

This letter is not from Ed McMahon. This letter is from a schemer named Mr. Mitch Klass, who offers to be my "new business partner" and who tells me the $95,093.35 check inside, made payable to me, might as well be real.

"Patrick Combs, I expected to hear from you by now. Take a close look at the check above. It's just a sample of the money you could be receiving soon."

Everything about the check looks *ultra*-real.

Bank account and routing numbers.

Signature.

Office of Treasurer.

Date.

Check number.

For **"the sum of $95,093dols35cts."**

Payable to my name.

With the words *"NOT NEGOTIABLE FOR CASH"* typed in the top right-hand corner.

A red headline says, *"We'll teach Patrick Combs how to make $95,093.35 in just three weeks! We took in that amount in just three weeks. Other mail boxes have also made HUNDREDS OF THOUSANDS OF DOLLARS!! In fact, your mail box, at 326 Carl Street, could be soon be STUFFED FULL OF CHECKS in varying amounts and FREE MERCHANDISE!! Now I've written to you several times before about an exciting new MONEY MAKING OPPORTUNITY. The one that said, 95,093.35 IN JUST THREE WEEKS!! The same one that was featured on TV! And frankly I'm surprised I haven't heard from you yet. Patrick, I know what you must be thinking, 'Is this for real?' Let me assure you, it is very real. There is a MULTI-MILLION DOLLAR market just waiting for you!!"*

Shut up—you had me at hello—I'll deposit it already. But seriously, the letter goes on and on for eight pages of continual references to BIG MONEY in ALL CAPS followed by at least half a dozen exclamation points. It's highly likely that Mr. Mitch Klass is the exclamation point's biggest fan.

Getting phony, come-on checks isn't new to me. They seem to come almost weekly these days. But all of them are not worth the paper they're printed on because of the words *"Not negotiable."* A funny choice of words, this "Not negotiable." Could it mean to say that you can't try and negotiate with your bank to get more money for the check—that the value of the check is set firmly at $95,093.35—take it or leave it?

Maybe it was that thought that got me thinking about how delightful it would be to deposit this fake check as a joke. Maybe it was just the thought that such a large deposit into *my* minuscule bank account is a joke in and of itself. At twenty-eight years old, my account balance is so low I often have to question what justifies me not just using a piggy bank. Five-year-olds usually have more money than me. And that's precisely why it seemed so damn funny to deposit a fake check for almost $100,000 into my bank account. It would be an unmistakably ridiculous deposit that for sure could only result in a teller's laughter. So off to do it I went.

PREPARE YOUR DEPOSIT

First, it is an odd sort of pleasure to key in a $95,093.35 deposit. I'm usually done keying in my deposit amount after three digits, but today that was only half way. So this is how the rich and famous feel at their ATMs. Their banking amounts are significant. Ironically, this is the first day my deposit amount doesn't feel like a joke. But I have not forgotten that my check isn't real, and so when it's time to endorse it, I do so without a signature, with only and simply a hand-drawn *smiley face*. I am proud of my mark; it screams good humor.

Then my attention goes to the scrolling mouth of the machine that is wanting to eat my check. I have a flash of doubt that the ATM will accept my fake check. Surely magnetic ink is being accounted for. I picture the ATM will choke on my check and spit it back like a vending machine rejecting an old dollar. Perhaps a light will then flash on the screen that says, "Bullshit!"

As the mouth of the ATM is scrolling and hungering, I have a moment of hesitation. Maybe the bank won't think it is funny. Yes, of course the bank will think it's funny. It's like depositing Monopoly money, and if that's not banker humor, nothing is. A teller will chuckle at the sight of the absurd fake check and then call me on Monday morning to say, "Mr. Combs, the check you deposited on Friday wasn't real..."

"Can you make an exception, just this once?" I'll ask.

And together we will share a laugh, a small bonding.

My fingers release their hold on the check, and the ATM eats it up like a cat licking cream.

I grab my deposit receipt and, for the first time ever, I walk away from my bank laughing. I have done good.

First Interstate Bank
"We Mean Business."

REALITY CHECK

My first indication that perhaps I was wrong came later that day from my wife, Lisa. "You did what? What did you do that for? You shouldn't have done that." We are recently separated, and reactions like this are part of the reason why.

Admittedly, I remember nothing else from Friday, May 19, 1995, the day of my prank deposit. There must have been nothing else to remember about it. My journal has nothing noted, my calendar nothing marked, so it must have been a completely ordinary day. The kind that almost doesn't matter in the big picture of your life. The kind of day that blurs together with all the other days when you wake up, shower for twenty minutes, work, eat—or forget to eat because of working—briefly talk to a friend over the phone, hope for sex, struggle with a relationship, daydream about your dreams, use the bathroom— and check the mail.

Since I'd also received credit card bills in the mail that day, it's a safe bet that I spent some time that day managing my debt. I manage $5,000 of monthly minimum credit card payments on a shoestring budget and keep interest rates down by moving $45,000 of debt around like a game of musical chairs. Whenever a new low, three-month introductory rate is offered by a different card, I move the money, or call and play credit card companies off one another in order to get better rates.

The only other thing I know about that day is that I worked at my home office desk on the speaking and writing profession I'd been working hard to establish for myself the past three years. The entrepreneurial endeavor was the reason that I had $45,000 of credit card debt. That, and perhaps the fact that the book I'd just had published for college students was being returned by bookstores *en masse*. Nonetheless, my career was hitting stride. I was speaking at colleges around the country about thirty times a year. My topic? Success, of course.

GOOD TIMES AT THE DMV

At Scott's house the music is blaring.

"This album is fucking awesome dude—listen to this!" he says as he pushes the volume even further. Furniture is shaking.

The woman singing is *pissed* off. Really, *really* angry. Anger-management angry. I like it. But the look on Scott's face—sort of gleeful and impish, like a teen about to show his friend a centerfold—tells me something contraband is coming.

"Who is it?" I yell.

"New artist, Alanis Morissette. Dude, I *have* to meet this woman. I am in love with this chick," he says, smiling through the very short beard that covers his very large cheeks.

"It sounds good."

"I've fucking got to meet her, bro. This chick has balls! I'm going to meet this woman!"

"You want to meet a chick with balls? You're in the right city...Scott, did I show you my new driver's license picture yet? Check it out."

Scott gives it a look and starts laughing.

"Patrick, *what the fuck*? When was your hair *this* long?"

"Never. I'm wore a wig for my picture. I even took my road test wearing it. How stupid do I look?! Good times at the DMV."

"You look like a stoner."

"Exactly!"

I'm no stoner. Never smoked pot. But I like taking funny driver's license photos. I met Scott because he drew a cartoon that I used in my book. He's a storyboard artist for Industrial Light & Magic. We have great conversations about music and our ambitions. I want to be a great speaker and he wants to be a great filmmaker. We're both confident we're going to make it. I drive a piece-of-shit car and can't afford a stereo, but I'm determined to make it as an inspirational speaker.

May 25

I have a pile of large envelopes that need postage, so I load them into the car and head first for the post office. I do this errand a lot. Each envelope contains a kit describing my speaking services. Each kit is a $2.90 mailing expense, but also a chance at booking a gig. I park my burgundy 1977 Ford Granada, nicknamed by my friends the "Gramamma," a block away from the post office, which also happens to be a block away from my bank. I hit up my ATM for $40 first. Out spit two twenties and a little orange and sand-colored receipt—which automatically tells me my bank balance because I think my bank wants me to kill myself. But my eyes are not prepared for what they're about to see.

$101,217.34

This is NOT my account balance...Bill Gates's perhaps, but...

Suddenly I remember the $95,093.35 deposit I'd made five days before—*oh my God, the bank cashed the phony check!*

$101,207.17 looks Lotto large to me. It looks like Fort Knox-sized numbers. It is a dollar amount that I think buys and pays for entire homes. *Trust me on that— I grew up in a trailer house.* $101,207.17 looks like all the money in the world. When I dream of big money, I dream of $10,000. $100,000 is not a number I yet conceptualize.

My body breaks out into the mad dash for home, forgetting completely that I had driven to the bank. The receipt is a Golden Ticket in my hand as I weave my way through the Haight-Ashbury neighborhood. I am talking to myself all twelve blocks. This can't be happening to *me*! This has to be a mistake. The check was fake. This can't be happening. It couldn't have been real. I'm rich. Holy mamma, God above, I'm rich! This is a mistake. I hope this is not a mistake. Please let me be rich.

Up the marble steps, down the hardwood hallway, straight to the phone hanging on the wall I run. I call my friend Michelle hoping she will do a small favor for me.

"Michelle, please call wherever you bank and tell them what happened to me—but don't mention my bank's name—and ask them how this could have happened. Then call me back!"

Michelle obliges. I plop into my swiveling office chair with no idea what to do with myself besides stare at the fantasy number on the little orange and white receipt and wait for her callback, which comes soon.

"Hi. Okay, my bank manager doesn't think there's been any mistake. They've just credited your account for the dollar amount, but the funds are on hold until your check clears or bounces. And he said your phony check is going to bounce in two or three days, four days max. Sorry."

"Really? That's it?"

"The guy I spoke to said you could have deposited a check written on the side of a *cow*, and they'd credit your account," Michelle says.

"Really? A cow?…Do you know anyone with a cow?" I say, trying to salvage some levity.

An incredible and Lotto-like thing has *not* happened to me. And it is only a matter of hours or days before my balance will return to a mere $5,000 tops, every dime of which is obligated to a truckload of "minimum payments." This sucks.

BACK TO REALITY

That night, tucked away in a lower Haight club that has the wing of a jet for its bar, Scott takes one look at my bank receipt and exclaims, "Shit, dude! What'd you do, rob a bank?" We are with other friends, and my $100,000 balance monopolizes the conversation. People fantasize about what they'd do with a $100,000 windfall: a '56 Thunderbird, a home, a charity, funding for a film, a sudden departure to Mexico. I know what I would do with it—I would use it for much-needed relief, pay off all my credit cards, make my speaking materials better, and bank the rest for my monthly expenses.

Before crawling into bed, I phone the twenty-four-hour banking line. A prerecorded woman's voice speaks as if happy to tell me, "Your account balance is...$100,350.33." *It is like phone sex.*

May 26th

It'll definitely be gone now, I tell myself as I pick up the phone to see if the money is gone. I'm sure it will be.

"Your account balance is...," says the automated gal, "$100,266.80."

I want to keep this girl on the phone for hours. I call her another ten times, and by 4:00 p.m., she is still whispering six figures in my ear.

May 27th

I have programmed the twenty-four-hour banking number into speed dial to save my fingers. Each time the automated teller—who is quickly becoming my significant other—romances me with the news that my account balance remains over $97,000. *This is nuts. It's been a week. That check should have bounced by now.*

I pull on some pants, throw on a T-shirt, return to my bank—and go in. I approach the young red-headed teller. She is smiling like sunshine, but I feel cold. My words pour out slowly and carefully. "I'm thinking of buying a home this afternoon. If a little later today, I need a cashier's check for $70,000, could I get the money?"

Of course I cannot. She will see a red flag or blinking light next to my name.

She types my account number into her computer, looks up at me, and declares, "Yes, the funds are available, Mr. Combs."

All I did was ask. And all she did was tell. But suddenly I feel criminal. And in danger. And most of all, excited beyond belief. My blink reaction is to get out of the bank, fast. I hope I said thank you and good-bye, but I cannot be sure. On the sidewalk I feel safer, and also very, very special. I have the world's greatest secret. And I am the world's luckiest man!

The money was still in the bank so that I could be safe from being thrown down and handcuffed. But out on the street, I'm calculating the risks of withdrawing the money and skipping to Mexico, where it would be worth twice as much. I figure that I could also take every cash advance available from my small chest of credit cards and suddenly be $150,000 liquid. Certainly *that* much money would go a *long* way in Mexico.

Take the Money and Run

I go to Scott's apartment and run my Mexico calculations past him.

"Scott, what you do think? Would *you*? *Should* I? Yes? No? *Maybe?* And if I am going to do it, I'd have to do it *pronto* because that money is not going to last. Any day, minute, or second now, they're going to discover the mistake and—snap—the money's gone!"

I'm talking *really* fast.

"Easy, boy! You're out of control. No, you don't touch the money. It's 'mistake money.' And it better be there when they notice it missing," Scott says.

*Scott doesn't get it because the money isn't in **his** account, but I cover for my upset.* "Yeah, yeah, you're right. You're right. But that money would buy a lot of fireworks and margaritas, would it not?" I blather.

"Ever since this money showed up in your account, it's *all* you talk about. It's all you *want* to talk about. My suggestion? Forget about this money, and get back to a real life," he counters.

I'm not sure I like Scott anymore. *Obviously he's just jealous.* I excuse myself, return home, and call for my bank balance.

For the next five days—every morning, every night, and every day—I speed dial for my automated teller. I need her to confirm my riches to me over and over again. With each passing day, I worry more that I might wake up and find myself once again ordinary. But my automated darling keeps speaking her words of love each time I call.

June 1st

Wednesday comes excruciatingly slowly. As I board a plane to attend a four-day speaker's conference in Orlando, I recognize that I need an intervention, so I swear off calling for my bank balance during my trip. I need the break from my addiction. For the first few days, the sight of a phone makes me jittery. I see ATMs everywhere I go. I don't make it an hour without thinking about the money. But gradually toward the end of the trip, I get back to my old self, the one capable of thinking of other things besides money.

When I return home Sunday night, it could be said that I am looking forward to the $95,000 being gone from my account. That I have discovered the virtue of normalcy. I call my automated girlfriend, anticipating the olden days of very little money in the bank. She purrs, "Your account balance is...$98,023.40." It takes a moment to register, but then I realize that the money is not just still there, but *I'm accruing interest!* My addiction is back and I couldn't be happier!

Another week passes torturously slowly, with the money remaining in my account. I am skipping meals to check my balance. I am not working. I am waking up early. I am not speaking to friends. I feel now that my life depends very much on the $95,000 still being available for withdrawal.

June 10th

I can no longer stand just leaving the money where it can be taken from me at any second. So, exactly three weeks after I had deposited the sample check, I decide to return to my bank. I enter wearing jeans and a T-shirt, a stark contrast to the suited older man with salt-and-pepper hair and wire-frame glasses who is ready to help me. His name badge says he is the branch manager. Trying to appear relaxed, I speak.

"I recently deposited $95,000. Now, I don't want to spend any of that money if there is the possibility of the check being returned. You wouldn't like that, and I wouldn't like that. So how long should I wait?"

He asks to see my bank card and begins nonchalantly keying in my account number. He puts his fingers up to the monitor and scrunches his face, a gesture tellers usually do that I've come to associate with a shocking lack of money in my account. "Here it is, $95,093.35, deposited on May 19."

With that, he drops his finger, looks up at me suspiciously, and says, "Hmm. Very interesting. Wait a second, Mr. Combs."

I don't move, but I feel like I should, and rapidly. Instead, I just stand there frozen, watching him examine his screen closely while punching a button here and there.

"Mr. Combs, legally...that check can no longer be returned. See, checks can't come back after ten business days, so you're safe to spend the money now—you're protected by the *law*."

I go blank. All gears grind to a halt in my head. He has definitely thrown a wrench into my mind. Because I do not know what to think or say. For the first time in my life, I am truly stunned speechless. Somewhere in my head, engineers are trying to remove the wrench and reboot the brain. But that will be a very slow process today.

"Really...Oh, okay then, thanks."

I am already backing up. *Holy mother of God.*

My body has decided to get out of the bank and is doing so when my brain reboots enough for its first thought since the crash. *I have to read this ten-day law for myself.* Suddenly, with shaky hands, I am grabbing every brochure and pamphlet available off the counter as I exit to safety.

At home, I wade through every line of the boring pamphlets, all the tedious small print, yet can't find the law he had referred to, or, for that matter, any of my rights. The brochure is titled "Your Banking Rights," but I can attest to the fact that there is not a single customer right on any of its eighteen pages. The bank should have titled it, "What Made You Think You Had Rights?" And just when I conclude that the brochure is a dead end, on the back page, at the very bottom, in small print, I see a sentence that says, "For more information contact the Office of Thrift Supervision."

Directory assistance has a phone number for the Office of Thrift Supervision. I call right away and a man answers the phone.

"Hello, Office of Thrift Supervision. Dan speaking, how may I help you?"

I tell him what had happened—skipping my last name and where I bank—and ask him to confirm the ten-day law my bank manager was referring to.

"There's no such thing as a ten-day law."

Really? *Shit.*

"Your branch manager was wrong,"

"Of course he was," I lament.

"It's a twenty-four hour law. It's known as the midnight deadline. Banks have by midnight of the following day to tell you that your check bounced, or you're safe to start spending the money."

"Do you promise?!"

"But I don't think that's what's going on here. The more important question in a matter such as yours might have to do with negotiability. I wonder if the check you deposited—you say it was sent to you in a junk mail and wasn't supposed to be real?"

"It was a fake check. It said "not negotiable," I explained.

"Hmmm. I wonder if it was a true negotiable instrument."

"Explain, please."

"The law specifies nine—I think it's nine, it's been a long time—nine or eight specific criteria that a check has to match in order to be a legally negotiable instrument."

"Uh-huh." *I have no idea where he is going with this.*

"I can't be exactly sure what they are, but perhaps the check you deposited was actually a negotiable instrument because it matched the nine criteria. That would explain why your bank accepted it."

My fake check might have been accidentally real? This I'd never even contemplated. I'd only guessed it might have been mistaken as real.

"What are the nine criteria?" I ask softly, trying to not appear too eager.

"I don't remember, to tell you the truth. Law school was a long time ago, but there's a law book called *Brady's*, I think, *Brady's Banking Law*. It will list the criteria. Hastings Law Library probably has the book."

KNOW YOUR RIGHTS!

There was no reason to delay. In a matter of minutes, I got off the phone, looked up the address for Hastings, grabbed my car keys, and headed out the door. This might change everything. If the junk-mail company had accidentally designed a real $95,000 check, I would find out today.

San Francisco supposedly has more cars than parking spaces. I circle many times around the park that is surrounded by stately City Hall, the opera house, and the majestic public library before I find a spot. Hastings is a modern-looking, three-story, red-brick building with smoked glass. I've never been to a law library before.

Hastings is more uniform looking than the public libraries I've been in. I push through the single waist-high security bar and ask a man at the desk where I might find the book *Brady's Bank Law*.

"If you mean *Brady on Bank Checks*, it's on that shelf over there," he says, pointing.

I scan the rows and rows of books, all devoid of any pictures on their covers, and finally find it. *Brady on Bank*

Checks—The Law of Bank Checks, by Henry Bailey and Richard Hagedorn. It is a big, thick, three-thousand-page book with a black cover. Nothing like the small, bright motivational books I am used to reading.

I sit on the floor, flip it open, and immediately know I am in trouble. At fairs there are vendors who write your name on a single grain of rice and apparently those same people have published this book. Flipping through it, trying to find the law I need, I can't even find the table of contents in the monstrous tome. The more I look through it, the more I think I am going to pass out from the frustration that increases with every legalese-crammed page.

I give up in defeat and return the torture tool to the shelf. I am no match for this book. I went to a state school. And this law library has chewed me up and spit me out.

But as I am exiting, I see it—a small, pocket-sized book with a colorful cover. The only reason I see it is because—for some reason—it is face out on the shelf. It is titled *Negotiable Instruments and Check Collection In a Nutshell. In a nutshell! God must love me.* I drop to the floor and flip open the friendly little book randomly to a page that, as if by magic, reads, "The Nine Criteria for a Negotiable Instrument." Judgment day has arrived.

My eyes progress through the essential criteria: must have a signature, must have a date, must have the words "pay to," must have an exact dollar amount, etc., etc. My check clears the first eight hurdles! Now all I have to do is clear the ninth hurdle. As for the fact that my check carries the words "non-negotiable" in the top right-hand corner—I am trying to ignore that little fun fact. I turn the page. There stands the ninth criteria. My final hurdle to great fortune. It says, "The ninth issue is whether people can create an instrument that matches the first eight criteria, and then avoid negotiability by declaring on the instrument that it is not negotiable."

*Holy shit. My situation exactly. And all I need is the answer **no**. No, you can't create a very real-looking check and then make it worthless just because you wrote "not negotiable."*

No.

No.

No. I need a "No."

I take a deep breath. The roulette wheel is spinning to a stop, giving me a fifty-fifty chance at a hundred grand. I begin reading the answer slower than any sentence I've read in my life. I'm only letting my index finger uncover one word at a time.

"The...

answer...

is...

I hold my breath and slide my finger to the right.

"...yes."

My soul has just left my body. All fantasies I had about the $95,000 fizzle on the library floor like a firework that fails to launch. My life sucks.

But then...I move my finger a micro-inch further and see a comma. "The answer is yes," *Yes comma. Comma what? I'm back in the game!*

I take another deep breath, get on my knees, make the sign of the cross, and beg for cash redemption. *Please, God. We probably don't talk enough, but please let this work out for me. I'm so tired of being poor. I'm so tired of $45,000 of credit card debt...I'll cut you in.*

I dare to slide my finger and read on. "The answer is yes, **except on a check**. A declaration on a check that it is not negotiable is ineffective."

I reasoned each word carefully, but it quickly sunk in. I was the luckiest SOB alive. The get-rich-quick company had accidentally designed a real check. *"Not negotiable" on an IOU ruins it. "Not negotiable" on a promissory note makes it no good. "Not negotiable" on a contract voids it. But "not negotiable" written on a check doesn't mean shit!*

Now the last financial favor I'll ever need is to borrow a little money from a girl sitting close to me in the library to photocopy what I had just read.

Money Changes Everything

I fly out of the library on gilded feet. A parking ticket is waiting to destroy my day, but it doesn't stand a chance. Twenty-eight dollars is now mere pocket change, a measly amount I can gladly contribute to the city's upkeep.

At home I phone my mother first. When I tell her the exuberant news, she sounds afraid. "Son, for $95,000, they'll kill you. Don't you dare spend a dime of that money."

I try to assuage her worry by saying, "Okay, but I was going to buy you a Lexus and fill it with presents."

After a contemplative pause, my mother replies, "Don't you spend any of that money—for at least a month." Geez, my mother sold me out for a Lexus.

Next I decide to phone my brother for his advice. Mike, a year and a half older, lives in Boston. Our respective cities were almost perfect metaphors for our differences. Boston, older and conservative. San Francisco, younger and adventurous. I'd turned to my brother for advice many times, but in this case I was hesitant. He always came through with smart suggestions, but this time I wasn't sure I wanted to hear the mature thing to do. I was basically forcing myself to consider the advice he'd most certainly give me: "Patrick, give the money back right away—and grow up."

I wasn't too far off. After hearing my situation, he asks, "Are we related?"

Then he says, "Legally yours or not, whomever is missing this money is going to come for it—at night, with guns."

His assessment makes me nervous. "Yeah, I think you're right, Mike. So what would you do?"

"I'd get it in cash."

This was a bonding moment with my brudder!

"Patrick, get the entire amount in cash and put it into a safe deposit box at your bank. Then they'll have to ask you to return the money instead of being able to take it back without a word. Picture walking into the vault, going behind the curtain, and opening a box full with $95,000 cash. It'll be fun to look at. How many times in your life are you going to have $95,000 cash in a safe deposit box that you can play with?!"

Apparently money makes my brother horny.

I like his plan. I'd have control over the money, but it would never leave my bank. Shortly thereafter, I begin calling First Interstate branches and asking about safe deposit box availability. I learn that the only safe deposit boxes available are "Slim Jims". All the medium and large size boxes are long taken and held by the rich of San Francisco, who apparently had a lot to hide. I don't rent a Slim Jim because I estimate that $95,000 would never fit in such a small box. I am wrong in my calculation, but nonetheless, the miscalculation prompts my next move.

The next day, I enter an American Savings Bank on Van Ness Avenue. I sit down at the desk of a bank official, and, as much as I dislike stereotypes, it's a small Asian woman who is greeting me in broken English. "Hi, can help you?"

"Could I withdraw $100,000 in cash—assuming, that is, I had enough in my account to cover it?" I ask.

"Nobody ever done that in fifteen years I working," she chuckles.

"But if I wanted to, can you get me that much cash?"

She chuckles again, but this time nervously. "We have to tell IRS and order four days in advance. But nobody ever done that."

"Really?" *I do not want IRS involvement.*

"Yes, we no keep that much cash on here," she continues. "The largest bill in circulation now is $100 bill. No more $500 bills in circulation. We have to report to IRS any cash withdrawals excess of $10,000—some people bad guys, trying to hide money."

"Oh—not me. Thank you for your time. I was just asking."

Her nervousness, the required procedures, the information that she'd never handled a cash request of my enormousness before—it all makes my $95,000 seem like *even* more.

June 13th

I wake up and decide that if I can't look at the $95,000 in cash, it will be almost as fun to see it as a cashier's check. The decision to attempt the five-figure transaction feels dramatic. I decide I will go to my bank's most impressive San Francisco location, the California Street branch, located in the heart of the skyscraper district. Cathedral ceilings, marble floors, towering columns, gold trim, and red carpet made it fit for *Lifestyles of the Rich and Famous*. I give my clothing careful consideration. Dressing up in a suit and tie would be like scheming, I conclude, since I almost never dress that way. Business casual would be too boring. Old jeans and a torn T-shirt would be like entering the bank with a sign that said, "Hey, brother, can you spare $95,000?" A part of me needs to dare the system to stop me—so Levi's and a Hanes athletic T-shirt it is.

Inside the regal building, it's immediately obvious that I am the only one of the twenty or so customers that looks like a skate punk. I feel my confidence drop. *They won't hand over a $95,000 cashier's check to me. They'll tell me they made an error.*

My turn at the teller's window comes too soon. I can't get past the feeling that in some way I'm about to rob the bank. I'm actually too petrified to ask the middle-aged woman on the other side of the marble counter for a $95,000 cashier's check. Instead I quietly ask for a piece of paper. On it I write "$95,093.35," and as I slide it towards her, I say, *"I'd like to get this amount in a cashier's check, please."*

Such a stupid fucking way to ask for my cashier's check. I might as well have said, "Don't even think of triggering any alarms." Sweat is pouring down my sides.

Without saying a word, she begins moving quickly to grab papers and forms, then rushes out the words, "You need to write me a check." She seems bothered and I am not thinking well. My heart is doing a drum roll.

"I've never gotten a cashier's check before. What are you asking me to do?"

"Write me a check for the same amount," she says.

Finally understanding what she was asking, I begin to write out the check. I had never written $95,093.35 out in words before. It seems to take forever. *Ninety-five thousand, ninety-three dollars and thirty-five cents.* It barely fits on the line.

Time seems to sit still while she prepares the cashier's check and gets the manager's approval, but then, like a miracle, she is sliding the gray check across the counter to me. I am ready to get the money and bolt. To get out of the bank. I reach to take it—and in the worst moment of my life—she is not letting go off the check. *I am busted. I am so busted.* She is locking eyes with me.

"What are you going to do with this money when you walk out those doors?" she says. Her eyes do not flinch.

"I don't know." *But I know I'm busted.*

She does not release her hold on the check. "Would you like to speak with one of our investment counselors right now?" she says, smiling. "They can suggest excellent uses for the money."

You almost put me into cardiac arrest.

"No, thank you. But you should get a raise."

It's beyond comprehension that I have a cashier's check in my hand for $95,000. I walk straight back to customer service, rent a Slim Jim, and soon get escorted into the vault. It should be noted that renting the safe deposit box for $150 almost emptied my bank account. Inside the vault, the bank teller slides out the box that will be my treasure chest and points to the curtain I can go behind for privacy. "No need," I say, as I peel off the pink duplicate and slip the gray folded check into the metal container.

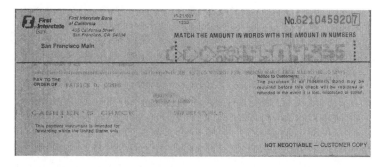

A huge smile spreads across my face as I exit the building. I am out of the bank and free. As I walk the street, just below the Transamerica Tower, I am endowed with the strange feeling that I am taller, swifter, and stronger. I feel like I have superpowers and could easily lift a large automobile off any person in distress. As I head to my car, I slip the safe deposit box key onto my key ring—a skeleton-like key now worth $95,093.35.

THE BANK FREAKS OUT

When I arrive home, I call my friend Michelle to tell her that I've managed to get a cashier's check. She has thus far loved hearing updates about the $95,000.

"You took the money? Why did you do that?" She sounds upset. "That's going to get you in big trouble!"

Her reaction scares me. Maybe taking the money was really stupid.

I decide to call Scott Edelstein, a trusted friend of mine in Minneapolis, for a second opinion. Scott was a long-distance friend I'd known for two years. He'd negotiated my book deal for me. I found him to be wonderfully wise, the only person I knew who could pepper a conversation with Zen stories. After hearing the whole chain of events, including Michelle's alarm, he says, "There's these two monks washing in the river when they notice a scorpion drowning. One monk scooped it onto the bank and got stung. He went back to washing and again the scorpion fell in. The monk again saved the scorpion, and again got stung. The other monk asked him, 'Friend, why do you continue to save the scorpion when you know its nature is to sting?' " "Because," the monk replied, "to save it is my nature."

I don't catch the drift of the story.

"Patrick, certainly many people will think what you've done is frightening and scary, but that's why they're not you. You're you precisely because you do things like this. Look at you. You launched your own speaking career without any training. You wrote a book because one day you got the inspiration to. A lot of people don't do things like that because of fear. I think it's fantastic that you deposited one of those junk checks. It's something everybody has fantasized about doing, but leave it to you to actually try it!" Scott's words, cheery and matter-of-fact, soothe my nerves and make me smile. "Just keep trusting your own instincts and you'll be fine."

We talk a bit longer, and then he adds, "I think you've got a story good enough for the national news."

I doubt there's a news story here and say good-bye.

Having the money in a safe deposit box alleviated my need to call and check my bank balance every minute. During the next week, I am able to focus on my speaking work. When the money does come to mind, I waver between wanting to keep it and fantasizing about donating it all to the Red Cross. The Robin Hood option appeals to me. I particularly love the thought of doing good with bad people's money. And I figured Mr. Mitch Klass, the man who sent me the fake check, was a bad person, preying on people with a get-rich-quick scheme.

I wondered a lot about what his reaction would be to my having successfully cashed his not-so-fake check. I knew the news of my windfall would reach him through his bank statement. And waiting for his reaction was an excruciatingly slow hell. His reaction seemed to be the only thing that stood between me and $95,000. And one day, after about a week, I got tired of waiting and wondering, and I decided to force the answer. Mr. Klass had included his phone number in the original letter he'd sent with the check, and I still had the letter. So I decided to call Mr. Klass and tell him what I'd done. Undoubtedly, he was going to call me soon, so it seemed better to act first. Better to catch him than to have him catch me. I dialed for my showdown. A woman answers.

"I'm calling for Mr. Klass."

"Have you purchased our $149 sales system?"

"I haven't."

"Mr. Klass can't take your call right now. He has to reserve his time for our sales associates, but if you want to leave a message, he'll try and get back to you."

"Hmm, okay. Would you tell Mr. Klass that I did get rich from his system—that I cashed the $95,000 check that came in the letter—the sample check."

"You cashed the check?"

"I did."

"And you got the money?"

"I did."

I must have said "I did" with perfect effect, because it prompted a long pause. "Hold, please, and I'll get Mr. Klass."

On hold I am treated to Muzak.

"Mr. Klass won't take your call, but he said to return the money to the bank, call the police, and have a nice day."

Was Klass going to call the police? Should I be worried? Or was he just going to ignore it? I decide to try and not worry about it. And to definitely *not* call the police. I feel a small laugh, very small, and slightly fake.

June 20th

Seven days after I put the cashier's check into the safe deposit box, and thirty-three days after I deposited the junk-mail check in the first place, I come home to two voice-mail messages from my bank. The first message is from the Haight Street branch of my bank, and the second voice-mail is from the bank's security department. Expecting these calls doesn't make them any easier to hear. And I am confused. I thought the calls would come from the get-rich-quick company, not from my bank. It's after 5 p.m., so I have to wait a day to find out why my bank was involved.

That evening, with my friend Scott standing by my side, I put my bank card into an ATM to get some cash for dinner. The ATM eats my card, and on the screen, green words glow: *Card Confiscated. Contact Your Branch Office Immediately*.

Looking over my shoulder, Scott says, "Oh shit, dude, you're going to San Quentin!"

"No, bro, I didn't do anything wrong. And as for con-
fiscating my ATM card, that's going to get me another
$5 for imperfect service."

I try to laugh it off, but it feels like the walls are closing in.

June 21st

I had a restless sleep and woke up before my alarm.
I caught an early-morning flight to New York to begin
a two-week vacation with friends and family. My flight
has a short stopover in Seattle at about 10 a.m., so I use
the time to make a phone call. I return the call from the
Haight Street branch of my bank.

"Sharon Kempner, please."

"Sorry, she's not in. May I ask who's calling?"

With the mention of my name she says, "Oh! Hold a
second, please."

Then another woman comes on the line and says, "You
got a cashier's check from us for $93,095.35 that we need
back. Can you bring me the cashier's check today?"

Like we're talking about a pen I accidentally took home.

"I'm sorry. I didn't get your name or job title."

"Sharon Kempner. Customer service manager. Can
you bring me that check?"

She sounds very nervous.

"I can't. I'm almost to New York."

Out the airport window a large Alaska Airlines jet
is rolling across a tarmac lined by pine trees. Sharon

interrupts me as I'm telling her the check is in a safe deposit box.

"Does anyone else have a key?"

"No."

"When do you come back?"

"I return July 6. I can give you the money then. But can you tell me how this matter came to your attention?"

"The check came back insufficient funds."

"Really? I was worried it might, but a First Interstate manager told me that, by law, it could no longer be returned."

Sharon snaps, "Well, that is wrong! It can come back for a full year. I'd like to know who told you that. Do you remember who it was?"

I do remember, but I protect the person's identity.

"What kind of check did you deposit?" Sharon asks.

"Have you seen the check?"

"I'm holding it in my hands," Sharon replies.

"It's a junk-mail check!"

I am happy to declare my good fortune.

"I thought that's what it was. Why did you deposit it? It clearly has the words 'non-negotiable' on it. Were you experimenting?" Sharon is baffled.

"I don't know."

I can't figure why they accepted it and now want it back.

"How do *you* think this happened, Sharon? That it was accepted for so long and then rejected?"

"I don't know, but you need to return the cashier's check. You shouldn't have done this." Frustration cracks her voice.

"I'll give it back when I return."

Apparently this was what Sharon had hoped to hear. "Well, yes. That will be the thing to do. Thank you."

I had read for myself that the junk-mail check was real, and a bank manager had told me I was safe to spend it. Yet now I was being told I had to return the money. I felt like I was being lied to.

A final boarding call over the loudspeakers alerts me to get back on the plane. Next up is a stopover in Chicago. Inside the cathedral-like airport that is O'Hare, I park myself at another pay phone and return the call from Owen Persons, First Interstate's security officer. A woman answers. At first, Owen Persons is not in, but upon hearing my name, he is suddenly available.

"Mr. Combs, I know you spoke with Sharon Kempner earlier, but I'm on the case now, understand? Here forth, you don't need to speak with anyone else but me. I want you to return that cashier's check immediately." He sounds as if he eats anger for breakfast. His words come at me with a truckload of force, enough to increase the speed of blood through my veins.

I want him to admit the check was real.

"Mr. Persons, I understand. Can you tell me how the bank could have cashed this junk-mail check?"

"I don't care a *bit* why First Interstate Bank cashed a junk-mail check. It shouldn't have happened. This is a matter of fraud on your part," he barks back.

It alarms me—the word *fraud*. Criminals on the post office walls commit fraud. FBI agents investigate fraud. Fraud gets you sent to jail. Fraud will kill my speaking career.

"I know you're out of town. Fly back right now and return that check!"

He knew I was out of town, but he didn't know that I was raised without a father figure and that I hated men trying to tell me what to do. My throat trembles two words:

"No, sir."

"Is there anyone here that can open the box for you?"

"No, sir, I'm the only one on the signature card."

"Then give me permission to *drill* the box."

I pause to let a lump move down my throat. "No, sir."

"So you won't cooperate?" his coarse voice spews.

I don't want to make an impulsive, stupid mistake. I can feel a bead of sweat running down my ribcage. My hand holding the phone is clammy. Before I can come up with a response, he yells again, "Why won't you give me permission to drill the box?"

"Because it would be irresponsible of me. This has all gotten really serious, really fast. Just give me a second here."

I am yelling. I struggle for a shallow breath, and then I let my words ride out on the exhale.

"I'll tell you what. I need this all in writing. Send me an official bank letter stating who you are and that the check was returned for insufficient funds."

He explodes into a machine gun of words.

"You're not getting any letter! This phone call is all you're getting. It's all I have to give you! You committed bank check fraud when you got a cashier's check for money you knew wasn't yours. This isn't about $100, or $10,000! You committed fraud to the tune of $100,000! If you don't return that money, what I'm going to give you is policemen on your door, young man! Now give me permission to drill open that box!"

I have to think fast. But I can't with all the flight announcements blaring, footsteps crashing, and hundreds of voices swarming. After a rush to judgment, I say:

"No, sir. You do not have permission."

Owen Persons says nothing.

While we hold the silence, I imagine that I am feeling the same fear fugitives feel as they try to get a flight out of the country.

"I haven't spent a cent of the money. And I have no intention of keeping money that doesn't belong to me Mr. Persons." *I privately think the money does belong to me.*

I catch a quick sigh from Owen. "All right then. I won't take further action, as long as you agree to call the minute you get home on July 6."

I say yes. Then he agrees to have my bank account unfrozen so that my checks won't bounce. Seemingly all is okay between us when the call ends. I ease into my airplane seat. Owen assumed the money didn't belong to me. That could be debated later. I feel relieved to have the call over, but the words *fraud* and *policemen* pound in my head.

FRAUD?!

I arrive in New York shook up and certain I need to know if I have really committed fraud. From yet another pay phone, a few quick phone calls to law schools back in the Bay Area give me a short list of lawyers who specialize in banking and checks. I call Manuel Fields first because he has twenty years of experience, specifically focused on check fraud.

Calling escalates my nervousness. For all I know, telling him all that has transpired might be a legal form of confession, further evidence that could put me behind bars. But I feel desperate. Was what began as a joke now a federal offense? Would I need a lawyer fast?

I tell Manuel my first name only, and then all that had happened. I ask him if I need a lawyer.

He lets out a quick laugh, then asks, "Exactly how much was this check for?"

"Ninety-five thousand."

For what has to be at least fifteen seconds, all I can hear is hard laughter, seasoned with a few Spanish exclamations like *"Aye, Mio!"*

"I'm sorry," he says when his hearty laugh finally peters out. "I've just never heard anything like this."

I imagine Manuel leaning forward, serious, at his desk. According to commercial paper law, the money is now legally mine, he says. "The way a bank invalidates a check is by serving the depositor with a timely notice of dishonor. They've only got forty-eight hours to tell you. That's from when they found out—not from when you deposited it. You say they told you thirty-three days after your deposit. That suggests they blew it. But we'd need some proof. Then again, maybe they did tell you within the forty-eight hours. We don't have a way of knowing either way.

"Fraudulent checks are a different manner," he continues. "But since you deposited the check thinking there was no chance it would cash, and without even endorsing it—you didn't commit fraud."

A tremendous relief washes over me.

Manuel has more good news for me. "Nor was getting the cashier's check an act of fraud. The bank assured you the check could no longer be returned. They told you it was your money."

Manuel had no way of knowing the wide-mouth smile he was putting on my face. Then the desire to stand up against my bank stirred in me. It had no right to accuse me of fraud. I was an honest person! The more I thought about the whole situation, the more it seemed like I was being played. Owen needed an out to cover for the bank's mistake. He needed a sucker, and he counted on me to play that role. It seemed like the bank was taking the side of the junk-mail company. Maybe Mitch Klass, good ol' Mr. "Return the money and call the police," had called up the bank, screaming, "You let some jerk fraud us out of $95,000! Get our money back or I'll sue you so fast you won't see it coming!" Maybe that was enough to make the bank jump. In either case, it felt unfair and made a letter from the bank seem even more important. I wanted to see what reason they'd state for my needing to return the money. It would probably be a lie.

I spend the evening visiting a good friend, Scott Wolfman, in New York. He knew about the junk check before I arrived, and loved it, but the latest chapter of fraud accusations soured him. "You're on very thin ice, Patrick. Maybe it's time to give the money back. What's more important—making a point with this junk-mail company, or your career and reputation?"

"Sure, I see what you mean." I change the subject. He doesn't seem to be into the principle of the matter.

That night I receive two back-to-back e-mails from Scott Leberecht, his response to the latest news.

From: (Scott Leberecht)
To: UpWinger@aol.com
Subject: Holy $93k Batman!

God Damn Patrick, you are fucking outrageous! I would have LOVED to hear the conversation with that security dick! The check is voided—yeah right, that's why there are trickles of sweat rolling down my fat ex-cop butt-crack! I'll be back July 6. I'll be back July 6. I'll give you the money back then. I FUCKING LOVE IT!!!!!

From: (Scott Leberecht)
To: UpWinger@aol.com
Subject: $93k

Didn't write as much as I wanted to the last time—got pulled away. Amazing Amazing Amazing. You must have the cockiest grin the world has ever seen right now. Why did you reassure security officer pee-pee pants that you weren't going to spend the money? Did his huffing and puffing get to you? You fucking pussy. Now what leverage do you have? You could have asked for anything! Now you look like someone that can be gotten to with mere verbal pressure! I know, I know, Deputy Dick was "ON THE CASE" Whoopee FRIGGIN' Doo. You know I'm just giving you shit, pal! You're playing them juuuuust riiiight. I think it's kinda weird how fast they all give off a sigh of relief after you simply SAY you'll return the money. I think you should try and get them busted big time for freezing your account. I think that is complete bullshit. Motherfuckers. I can't wait to hear the next installment of "The Price is Right" with our favorite host Patrick Combs!!!!!!

June 24th

The next day, I travel to Boston and visit my brother Mike, his wife, Anne, and my mother. The bank's threatening call disturbs them. Mike, who I really hope will understand the principle behind my actions, just shakes his head and says, "What are you holding out for, Pat? You're going to give the money back, so why not just give it back now?"

"I'm holding out for a simple letter admitting they made a mistake! God, an official letter for my files is so little to ask. And for the junk-mail company to politely ask me for the money back like you and I discussed. They screwed up. They could at least say thanks for not spending it all."

"But you're gonna give it back?"

"Yeah, sure, unless the junk-mail company decides to treat me rudely. Legally, the money is mine now. I don't *have* to give it back."

My brother's eyebrows scrunch the same way they always did when he disapproved. "Hey, Anne and I are wiring the house with Ethernet connections in every room. Wanna see the hub? It's in the basement, along with my Batman collection. Anne got tired of action figures taking over everywhere." Mike was a mild-mannered technology manager by day, and a Batman fanatic by night.

Later, I find myself alone in the kitchen with my mom. From her seat at the table, rubbing her hands together for comfort, she says, "Patrick, you better not spend a cent of that money. I worry your bank's going to get meaner and meaner."

"I won't spend a cent."

"They'll throw you in jail, son. People get mean over money. You don't believe me, but I know. So you be very careful, son."

"I'll be careful. Don't worry, Mom."

"That's what I do. I worry about you boys."

That night I receive an e-mail from Scott Edelstein.

CommConSE

Re: $95,093.35

UpWinger

WOW! You've got a fascinating story—one which I am sure will become even more fascinating when you return on 7/6. I am VERY interested in what will happen. Keep me posted. I am particularly interested in the following: 1) If there had been over $95,000 in the junk mail sender's account, WOULD the check have cleared? The check was NOT returned for being a non-negotiable instrument. THE SYSTEM FAILED AT EVERY TURN. The error was caught for an UNRELATED reason. 2) Why the frig it take so long to be returned? 3) I wonder what bankers can actually do to you if they want? I can't believe they have the right to drill into any safe deposit box they want without a court order. That sounds like a simple bogus threat. But it interests me that the banker would make it, KNOWING it's bogus. I also can't believe that a bank can, whenever it pleases, claim that a cashier's check it wrote was no good, and can say, "We fucked up, so YOU legally owe us for the check whenever we say so." Sounds like everything he was doing was total lie and bluster. Actually, it's probably a blessing that the folks in Ohio are out of the loop. And there still may be quite a news or feature item here—maybe a BETTER one than if the Ohio outfit had taken the loss. Thanks for keeping me up to date.

June 25th

The next day, I phone my bank's general customer service number and request a photocopy of the original junk check. I feel I must have it to be able to see clearly that my check matched the nine criteria. For the person who takes my order, it is business as usual. I will receive it in a few days by mail.

The letter arrives on schedule and I have a friend open it and read it to me over the phone. It is a photocopy of someone else's check for $6.71. I am pissed. It could have been a simple mistake, but it seems like the bank is trying to keep me from having a copy of the check. Without it, I can't confirm that the check matched the nine criteria making it legal.

Sitting at my brother's desk, I am about to resort to an option that I dread: calling Owen Persons, the security officer, and asking him to fax me a photocopy of the check. I imagine him exploding again, but I see it as a necessary move. I am about to pick up the phone when my mom pulls up a chair. Although my mother is exactly as she often describes herself, "tubby little cubby all stuffed with fluff—like Winnie the Pooh," she was never to be underestimated.

"Patrick, why are you calling the security officer? Haven't I taught you to deal with VIPs? Call the president of the bank."

"It's not just a bank, Mom. It's a giant corporation with an international CEO."

"Well then, call that person. You're not a criminal, so you don't need to talk to the security officer. You call the CEO. Haven't I taught you to go to the top?"

"Yeah, you have," I say, humbled by my mom's wisdom and appreciative of her support. She sits there with me as I make the calls.

It takes several calls to learn that the CEO's name is Bill Siart. When I try to reach him, I am told that he doesn't take any calls personally and that I'd have to go through the Consumer Affairs Department. I reach the manager of the department and tell her that I have a problem with my branch office, and I'm having a lot of trouble speaking with anyone who wants to help me handle this problem fairly.

"I'll gladly help you any way I can," she replies in a courteous voice. I request a photocopy of the front and the back of the check and the official letter from the bank requesting the money back from me. When I tell her that Owen Persons had denied me the letter, she says, "Oh, Mr. Persons is our *senior* security officer, highly regarded, and twenty-two years with the bank. But I will call him and see what he can do."

June 28th

After the weekend, I am back at my computer in my brother's small home office, checking my e-mail. Then the fax fires up. Out of the machine comes the check copy. More detailed than I had remembered, it certainly matches all nine criteria for a negotiable instrument. It is more real-looking than any of my family had ever imagined.

Next, the fax machine spits out a memo from First Chicago Bank – not First Interstate and not a bank I've ever used. It does not have my name on it anywhere. It does have the amount of the check, $95,093.35, on one line, the word "non-negotiable" circled on another, and the name and phone number of an account adjuster at the bottom. Mike encourages me to call the number. "At this stage in the process, you're negotiating with the bank now for a copy of the letter. In negotiations, the person with the most information usually wins."

My family sits down for lunch while I phone the account adjuster, a man named Michael Bickham. I tell him I'm holding a memo from him dated June 5 and wondering if he can explain it. He asks for a few reference numbers off the paper and then says, "It's the notice of dishonor our bank sent to First Interstate about the $95,093.35 check. On the same day, we also reclaimed the money from First Interstate."

"What's a notice of dishonor?"

"It's when we notify your bank that the check they gave us was bad, and we reclaim our money."

"So my bank is out the money?"

"Yes," he confirms.

Before I can consider how I feel about my bank losing the dough, it hits me. The burning question raised earlier by Manuel was now answered. June 5 was the day my bank learned that the check had been dishonored. But June 21 was the day it had notified me. It had missed its legal, twenty-four hour midnight deadline by sixteen days—and then accidentally faxed me a memo that proved it! And it seemed like the memo came from Owen Persons himself, because the fax line at the top said "FIB Security." Owen must have thought that by faxing this document, he was satisfying my desire for a letter that proved the check had bounced. Instead he'd faxed me the smoking gun. I'd have to give him $5 for that mistake.

At the end of our conversation, the account adjuster not only obliges my request for the name of the other bank my check routed through, he tells me who I should ask for and what item number I should reference. I race to make my next call. The woman responds to me with a candor she probably reserves for fellow bankers. I scrawl notes onto a yellow pad of paper as she relates the entire history of the check's movement through the banking system. The bank received my deposit on Friday, May 19. On Monday, May 21, it was overlooked by First Interstate and sent on to the bank in Chicago that was acting as a clearinghouse. It was again overlooked there. The next day, May 22, it was sent on to the Federal Reserve Bank in Cleveland, Ohio, and this bank rejected the check immediately, calling it a "non-cash" item. The check was then routed to her bank in Cleveland, because that's where the Association of Certified Liquidators had its account. She said her bank sent a notice of dishonor immediately to the bank in Chicago, on June 4.

As I look over the ill-drawn map of my check's path across the United States that I had just scrawled on the yellow pad on my desk, I am bewildered as to why my bank had delayed for sixteen days in notifying me that my check bounced. Apparently, somebody at my bank was smoking crack.

I make the first entry about the $95,000 check into my journal:

No wonder my bank won't send a letter; there's nothing they can say in it! They can't say the check wasn't real without lying on paper. They're way past being able to officially notify me of it bouncing. So they haven't a legal leg to stand on. And I guess it never crossed their minds to just call me, admit their mistake, and ask for the money back nicely. Why would they? They never let customers out of mistakes. It's a $25 service charge whenever someone accidentally bounces a check, no matter what. But now, with the tables turned, instead of them paying for their mistake, they try and get the money back with bullying and lies. Screw them. I'm keeping the money if they want to act like this.

I wake up a few days later to an e-mail from Scott Edelstein, a response to the latest update.

CommConSE

Re: $95,093.35

UpWinger

The plot continues to thicken nicely. PLEASE keep me updated. Since you asked my opinion, I'll give it. I don't think you should keep the money under ANY circumstances, for several reasons. Give it back and tell the media. You'll be an American hero for both

1) beating the system, which everyone dreams of doing, and 2) actually giving the money back, which Americans, being more honest and decent than we give ourselves credit for, will adore. I say go for the heroism, NOT the bucks. Furthermore, if you do go for the bucks, be assured that the bank will be more than happy to do what it can to ruin your life with lawsuits and threats and general assholiness. Why set yourself up for such crapola, especially since you don't have to? Give them their money, let the media go wild, and you'll come out famous AND smelling like a rose—and everyone else will be happy, to boot. Why hire a lawyer or a PR firm? They'll just take some money from you. Break the news to a few national media on your own—e.g., *USA Today*, *Wall Street Journal*, *People* magazine, and a couple of the TV networks. I do NOT suggest the following, though it would certainly be interesting: keep the money, and use it ALL to purchase First Interstate stock. Show up at the next F.I. stockholder meeting and be vocal. Also, dress up as Elvis.

I don't sleep well for a week. I lie awake trying to decide if it really is worth it, continually trying to figure out my next move. I also worry about fraud charges, a lawsuit, court battles, jail time, and the disruption of my career as a speaker. I picture myself phoning a future client explaining that I'm on parole or trying to explain away the jail time. Not good.

July 6th

July 6 rolls around sooner than I care for. This is the day I had promised Owen Persons that I'd return to San

Francisco with the check. However, I have decided to skip my flight, call Owen Persons, and demand the letter, with three thousand miles of distance between us. I plan on giving him an ultimatum: hand over a letter to my liking, or never see the money again. Good plan, except that all I can imagine is that Owen may simply respond in a calm and collected voice, "Yeah, see you in jail, punk." End of call, end of my life. I wake up nervous and remain so all day as I put off the dreaded phone call.

My battle with the bank over the principle of the entire matter isn't worth the anxiety eating away at my life. It might get me jail time. Even the idea of fighting so that the money could go to charity was losing its luster. It would be like giving away ill-gotten gains. The money wasn't *meant* to be mine. Family and friends had already indicated they'd just give back the money and forget the letter. They were all people I trusted. Yet, a part of me thought I was right and the bank was wrong. And it was me who would have to roll over if I backed down.

Finally, at 9:30 p.m., I sit down at the kitchen table in front of the phone, planning out exactly what I will say. I will play hardball. No more Mr. Nice Guy.

To my surprise, my brother wanders by. He gives me some help with my script. "Overdemand," he recommends. "That's what good negotiators do. At some point it will make him say, 'I can't do all that for you—what do you really want?' "

Then my mother sits down across from me. She wrenches her hands together, then rubs her arms without saying a word. I hope she can't see how afraid I am, so I focus on the notes in front of me and try to calm my breathing. Before I know it, the clock on the stove reads 10:55 p.m. Owen won't be at work anymore, but I have his pager number. If I am going to do this, I have to do it now.

I ring Owen's pager and punch in my brother's phone number. Then I sit back and wait for his call.

My hands dampen with sweat. The muscles of my neck tighten. I fight off a tiny, and completely unusual, twitch on my right cheek. I give a fake reassuring wink to my mom. I've never before been this scared.

Rrrrrrriiiiiiiiiiiinnnnnnnnnggggggggg! The phone sounds like an alarm. I give a quick glance to my mother. Despite the tight feeling in my chest, I am able to speak my first words with strength.

"Hello, Owen. It is July 6, and I'm contacting you as I promised, but I've extended my stay in Boston. This call is to inform you that upon my return, I don't intend to give the money back unless we reach a different agreement. Let me explain why."

He tries to speak but I cut him off.

"I've received no official notices from First Interstate making a legal claim to the money. And no one has explained to me why I should give it back. Everyone, except you, has advised me that the money is legally mine. I was told by a First Interstate teller that the money was safe to spend because a law protected me from it coming back after ten days. I've been advised that, according to commercial paper law, the money became mine when First Interstate didn't serve me with a timely notice of dishonor. And that a check is not made non-negotiable by printing the words 'non-negotiable' on the front. Now, unless we reach some other agreement, I'm going to keep the money."

I just know his next words are about a warrant for my arrest. That he'll see me in court.

"Patrick, I like you. Perhaps we got off on the wrong foot in the first conversation. Where do we go from here?"

Oh, no, Mr. Persons, I felt the love in the first call.

I tell him my dissatisfaction about being treated like a criminal, rather than a twelve-year, good customer. Pissed because my bank account was frozen. Mad because the confiscation of my automatic teller machine card forced me to have to borrow money. And most of all, outraged for being stiff-armed over the simple request for the letter.

Owen apologizes respectfully and promises to get me an official letter from First Interstate. He says he will look into trying to get my ATM card replaced and politely tries to counter my legal claims to the money. "I can appreciate the laws you're citing," he says, "but none of them apply because what you deposited was an advertisement. Trust me, I have twenty years in banking, and a law book called *Brady on Bank Checks* sits right here on my desk as a reference."

I say nothing, wondering if he is right.

My mom makes tea as Owen and I speak for half an hour. I calmly and firmly reassert my rights, and Owen politely tries to explain them away. He never makes a single request of me—he doesn't even ask when I will return to San Francisco. He never uses the words "fraud" or "criminal." We even find a common ground for agreement about the belief that companies who advertise using real-looking checks should be held accountable for them.

The call is over. With my arms stretched out wide, I take in a deep breath and let a smile take over my face.

"Tomorrow, or the next day, they're going to fax me the letter and this whole thing will have a happy ending," I exclaim to my mom. Relief washes over her face, and I stand to turn off the kitchen light.

July 9th

Three days later, Owen still hasn't faxed me the letter he had promised. It is time to head back home, and my mother and I wait in Boston's Logan airport for my flight back to San Francisco. My mother lets go of her grip on my hand to wipe her eyes. "Well, I won't tell you to stop doing things like this, because when you stop taking risks, life gets boring. Just keep saying your prayers, son, and I will, too." I do not know it yet, but this will go down as one of the most memorable moments I've ever had with my mother.

HENRY BAILEY

Back in San Francisco, days pass without a word from my bank. No fax. No letter. No call. No nothing. A team of their lawyers, I imagine, is working furiously, building a case against me, creating mounds and mounds of paperwork to send me to jail. On the other hand, there is a slim chance that they had simply decided to write the money off as a loss, and for that reason I don't call them. If that was their decision, I don't want to interfere. But more so, I worry more and more that the little I knew about bank check law will come back to hurt me, in a big, life-altering, irrevocable, permanent-record sort of way.

July 14th

My concern drives me back to the Hastings Law Library. Either my determination or a cup of coffee makes the difference. This time, I am better able to decipher a lot of laws within *Brady on Bank Checks* that seem to give me a legal right to the money.

I photocopy laws. I photocopy court cases, including one that holds it illegal for a bank to cancel a cashier's check. Then, just before my brain goes to mush and my change runs out, a fascinating footnote catches my eye. It is about the law that makes the words "non-negotiable" meaningless on a check:

1. The only problem with this approach is the use of blank sample check forms that bear language such as "void" or "non-negotiable" or "sample form" that is clearly intended to show that the particular sample or form is not intended as a valid check. Would potential liability exist if such a sample form is filled in without authority and passed to one who could take as a holder in due course? The 1990 provision might well be drafted to avoid such a possible problem.

It takes me a couple of reads to realize that the authors of *Brady on Bank Checks* saw my junk-check snafu coming. I note from the back of the book that both the authors of *Brady* were once professors at Willamette University. I'm suddenly on fire with the idea that if I could call and reach one of these two professors, Henry Bailey or Richard Hagedorn, the leading authorities in the land on bank check law, I'd finally get to the bottom of whether I have a legal leg to stand on, or a future appointment in a maximum security prison. The footnote about "non negotiable" language seemed like my perfect in. They would most certainly enjoy hearing about my situation. Right up their alley.

I call Willamette's Law School as soon as I get home.

"Willamette Law School. How may I help you?" says a woman's voice.

"I'm calling for Henry Bailey."

"I'm sorry, Mr. Bailey has retired."

Damn.

"Oh, then could I please speak to Richard Hagedorn?"

"Mr. Hagedorn is on sabbatical for six months. Would you like to leave a message?"

"No, I'm going to be some prisoner's girlfriend by the time he gets it."

"Excuse me?"

"Sorry, I didn't mean to say that out loud."

I am about to give up in frustration when an idea pops into my head. *There's got to be a way to get her to tell me where Henry Bailey retired to.*

"I wonder if Henry is enjoying his retirement?"

"Yes, he is," comes the reply in a warm voice. "As a matter of fact, he still keeps in touch with us on occasion."

"I'm from Oregon myself—Bend. I bet he retired to the beautiful state of Oregon."

"No, actually he retired in Providence, Rhode Island."

Within seconds, directory assistance is giving me a phone number for Henry Bailey in Providence, Rhode Island.

My orange cat sits on my keyboard, demanding my attention as I dial the number and let the phone ring. Hobbit purrs and drools as the ringing continues in my ear. As my mind drifts onto the cat's tenacious, never-ending attempts to be on the keyboard when I work, I forget I am even on the phone listening to ring after ring after ring. An elderly woman's voice snaps me out of my trance.

"Who is it?"

"Patrick Combs. Is Henry Bailey there?"

"Just a minute," and then I hear talking, accompanied by slow footsteps coming towards the phone. A few seconds later the phone connection is ended. *Did he just hang up on me?*

I redial the phone immediately, but it is not being answered. I know someone is there, so I let the ringing continue for what seems like the length of ringing bells at a high school fire drill. Finally, an elderly man answers. He is pissed like an angry Gene Hackman, only angrier. "Who is this?!...What are you calling about?!...Who are you?!!" He bombards me with questions but leaves only enough time for one-word answers. "Are you a lawyer?!...Are you a banker?!...Are you with the press?!... Then why the hell are you calling me?!"

It is now obvious why he retired. And to think that minutes ago I was picturing a friendly, bonding call.

I try to explain that I am calling because of a problem he had foreseen and footnoted, but he doesn't seem to care—until I mention the UCC code about the words "non-negotiable." There is a sudden focus and interest in Mr. Bailey's voice.

"Yes, I wrote about that problem in *Brady*, and I published an article about it in *Banking Law Journal*. It was never like that in the 1962 code."

"I deposited a junk-mail check and my bank cashed it..."

Henry cut me off before I could utter another word, angry again. "Well, it sounds like you weren't being very honorable."

"I deposited it because I thought my bank would never accept it—just as a joke—but they did and cashed it."

"Well, that doesn't necessarily make you a holder in due course." *Cantankerous*, I believe is the word my mother would use to describe people like Henry Bailey.

"Mr. Bailey, after cashing my check, my bank didn't tell me my check was no good for thirty-three days. So this money is legally mine, right, because of the midnight deadline?"

"Not necessarily. What you deposited wasn't a real check. You said it was a junk-mail check, right? What do you mean a junk-mail check? You mean one of those advertisements, come-ons, that try and fool you into thinking you won money?"

"Yes, sir. Exactly. Like Ed McMahon sends."

"Did the check have a name on it?" he says, becoming almost civil again.

"Yes, sir, it had my name on it."

"Your name!" My answer surprises him. "Hmm. Well, did it have a signature on it?"

"Yes, sir, an authorized signature and an account number," I say, feeling encouraged as I put my cat back down onto the floor.

"You're kidding. Sounds like these dummies deserve it."

I can hear the delight in his voice. Henry Bailey is out of retirement!

"Did it say 'Pay to the Order' on it?"

"Yes, sir."

"Well this sounds *good*."

"How much was it for?"

"Ninety-five thousand."

"Oh this sounds *really good*! Well when did the company call you?"

"They didn't, sir. The *bank* called me. They said the check was returned as a 'non-cash item.'"

"When did you deposit the check, and when did your bank notify you?"

"I deposited it on May 19th and my bank called me to say it bounced on June 21st. So the money is legally mine, right?"

"Well, that doesn't mean your bank missed the Midnight Deadline." he growled, chastising me with his voice. "They could have found on June 20th that your check bounced hence why they notified you on June 21st, well within their legal limit. You'd have to have an internal document from your bank proving they found out your check bounced before June 19th. So unless you have this internal document—this smoking gun—which I'm sure your bank isn't just going to hand over to you, son, you haven't got anything. So how else may I help *you* waste time during *my* retirement?"

"They faxed it to me, sir."

"What? What did they fax to you?"

"My bank faxed me the notification memo they received on June 5th from First Chicago Bank that informed them my check bounced."

"They did? Why in the *hell* would they do that?"

"I guess to show me my check bounced."

"Idiots. Well if your bank delayed that long, and you have this memo, you have a legal claim to that money. Your bank has to meet a Midnight Deadline! You need to get a lawyer because that money is legally yours. What did you do with the money son?"

"Well, sir, I got the money in a cashier's check and locked it in a safe deposit box at my bank, and now my bank is telling me..."

"You got the money in a cashier's check? Did you get that cashier's check for the exact same amount of money as the check you deposited?"

"I did."

"No, I mean right down to the penny!"

"Yes, sir, right down to the thirty-five cents. Why?"

"Why? Because you got this bank by the balls!" he exclaimed in a crescendo.

It's a very funny thing hearing "by the balls" when you don't see it coming. I had underestimated the source. Again, this is not a man you fuck around with. Apparently he went into law because he embraced the law's ability to bring the biggest of men to their knees, with a simple squeeze on the right legalities.

"Mr. Bailey, do continue."

"That's called Finality of Payment. In the history of courts and banks, anytime a bank has issued a cashier's check for the exact same amount as a recent deposit it accepted, the court has figured that bank knew exactly what it was doing and ruled in your favor every single time, son. So don't let this bank screw you around. Get a lawyer, because that money."

I didn't see the next line coming. But I felt it went a long way towards expressing Mr. Bailey's opinion of a vast majority of his peers.

"And don't get one of those lawyers on TV—the ones who chase ambulances! You need a real lawyer—a lawyer who understands bank check law."

I like Henry Bailey, like his fire. I offer him a compliment. "I appreciate your having co-written a law book so well that even I could understand it, Mr. Bailey."

I think he is going to respond with a thank you, that we are about to share a warm moment between friends.

"I didn't write it to be used by laymen. I wrote it to be used by bankers and lawyers," he barked back.

Henry has the last word. He says he is glad I had called to tell him.

Owen Persons had rested his claims against me because Henry Bailey's book resided on his desk. I was now going to rest my claims against the bank because my friend Henry said I was holding the bank's balls. It was certainly an enormous confidence boost; however, I can't get myself away from daunting thoughts about a large legal fight with a very angry bank. I worry that even if I did use the entire $95,000 to defend my legal rights, $95,000 of legal funds against a bank—a repository of millions of dollars—would be like fighting a fire hose, with a water pistol. I feel I need another way to stand up against this bank.

THE WALL STREET JOURNAL

July 15th

I recall my friend Scott Edelstein's suggestion that I had a news story on my hands. Originally, I took his comment as flattery. Today, it seems like a good defense. I'm thinking the bank might think twice about picking a fight with me if the news was watching. At the same time, I can't decide whether or not to tell my story to a newspaper. I worry a news story might make me look bad. I knew already that some people found the idea of depositing the check in the first place as immoral. Dark places in my mind script headlines like *"Motivational Speaker Bilks Bank for $95,000."*

I take my friend Scott Leberecht for a pizza to see what he thinks. We sit at a booth near the window that looks out onto Irving Street, where orange and white Muni trains rattle by regularly. Scott rushes pizza into his mouth, his eyes widening as I speak of possibly telling my story to the media.

"They might paint you as a criminal, but they might not. Either way, this story could spread like wildfire," he says while swallowing a mouthful of crust. "I could see the whole city talking about this dude."

Scott's eyes are on fire with excitement. Obviously he doesn't understand the possible downside for me personally.

"Yeah, maybe, everyone loves this story. But what about my reputation? 'Motivational speaker' and 'bank fraud' just don't sound good together."

"The thing is, you're not a criminal. You didn't do anything wrong."

"Right. Right. But nobody's gonna think that if the newspaper makes me seem like a criminal. And a lot of people think it was wrong of me to put the check in as a joke. A lot of people think I was scamming in the first place."

"That's the risk you'd be taking," Scott says, before taking a gulp of his cola. "But most people don't think you've done anything wrong, right?"

"But do newspapers think like most people?"

"I don't know, but don't bring fraud up and they probably won't either."

I pick up my glass and take a gulp of cold water. I tell Scott that it's inevitable that the media are going to ask me what I'm going to do with the money, because that's what everyone asks. I tell him I've got an idea of how to respond.

"Run it by me."

"How about I say that when the bank gives me the letter, I'm going to give the money back to the bank with the condition they donate every cent to charity?"

"That's a good idea, but I've got a better one. Ready for this?" Just then, our server, a young woman with a pierced nose and hair tinted green, interrupts us.

"Sorry to disturb you. You look like you're plotting to take over the world or something—but do you guys want anything else?"

Quickly we decline and get back to our conversation, but now Scott speaks more softly. "You've got to leave the reporter guessing. Just conclude with the fact that you've got the money in a safe deposit box and the law in your favor—reveal nothing else. That forces a story without an ending, leaving everyone wondering and fantasizing about what they'd do if it was them."

I knew a great idea when I heard one. But I shuddered over how easily it could backfire.

"A lot of people will assume I'm going to keep it, and hate me for it."

"Maybe, but with a story like that, a shitload of a lot of people will be on your side."

We *were* plotting to take over the world. At least that's what my body told me.

I leave the pizza parlor, walking west toward my apartment. I am in my own world, unaware of the people I am passing, swirling with fantasies about a big news story and fears about it backfiring. The fact that a paper might not even want the story doesn't cross my mind. By the end of the eight-block walk, I envy Scott's position: able to live vicariously through me, getting to think up the wild ideas without having the vulnerability of executing them. As I unlock my door, I doubt my willingness to phone a reporter. The possibility of an unfavorable article that I can never take back is just too great.

Words spreads fast that I might call the news. Lisa calls me and says, "I told Amy that you might call the paper and she said, 'This isn't the kind of story he should be proud of. He doesn't get it—the whole thing makes him look really bad.' " The insult makes me feel awful. If that's how an acquaintance felt, total strangers would probably judge me even more harshly. This insecurity, along with the fear I have about my bank attacking me, makes for a really shitty seventy-two hours.

July 18th

I need some kind of getaway. I cross the city by train to Ocean Beach. I walk along two miles of coast listening to Bruce Springsteen's *Lucky Town* CD on my DiscMan. I see the sparkles that appear in the sand moments before the ocean returns to the sea. Dogs run past me, chasing waves. Hang gliders pass over my head. A state of peacefulness I have not felt since May 24 washes over me. It would end up being the best day of my entire year.

As I walk barefoot on the beach, I try to decide what the check incident means to my life. Is it the universe's way of giving me the money I need? Or a chance to change the law about junk checks? None of the possibilities grab me, but the more I breathe in the peaceful, salty air, the more I feel I can trust the feeling that I haven't done anything wrong. I should call the newspapers. If people judge me differently after the article, it would be because they're different people with different values and different worldviews. It wouldn't mean I was bad or wrong.

I sit on the sand and in my mind go through all the newspapers I knew of. The *Enquirer* would almost certainly take my story because of its' sensational nature, but I feel I need a paper with more credibility. I think of a paper with enormous prestige, the *Wall Street Journal*. I just stupidly think, "If I'm in the *Enquirer*, I'm trash by association. If I'm in the *Wall Street Journal*, I'm credible." In thinking it through so little, I overlook the first rule of news: the more prestigious the paper, the more hard-hitting the journalism.

July 19th

It turns out the *Wall Street Journal* has a San Francisco bureau. A woman answers the phone, and I ask to speak to a reporter who writes features, explaining I might have a great story.

"What is it?" she asks. I figure that I will need to sell her on my story before she'll put me through to one of the reporters, so I launch into a brisk and upbeat telling.

I'm waiting for her to interrupt me and say "Okay, I'll see if any reporters might be interested in this sort of story." But she lets me of the big mouth go on and on.

And when I am finally finished, I wait to see if I have stimulated her desire to tell one of the reporters about me. But somehow I just know I've done the whole "pitch a story" thing all wrong. I've said too much. She probably had me on hold for most of my blathering.

"That's a great story! I'd love to write it."

"You're a reporter?"

"Yes, I am. Hmmm, there's one consideration though. If we run this story, there's going to be a lot of people who will try to copy what you did. Let me think about that, and I'll ask my editor if I can take this assignment. Call me tomorrow. I'm Sharon Massey."

Hobbit is again sitting on the keyboard. "Hobbit, you handsome orange hairball! If the *Wall Street Journal* can't make a fast decision, I say we give our story to the *New York Times*!" Swept up in confidence, I call the *Times*, but this time I can't get past the receptionist. "I'll pass your message on and see if any reporters are interested in your story. Thank you." And with her hang-up, the *Wall Street Journal* feels like a huge fish that might slip off the line. I gather photocopies of the check and all the photocopies I'd made of the laws, and I jump into my car.

The San Francisco office of the *Journal* is located on the eleventh floor of a skyscraper one block from where my cashier's check is locked safely away. I take the elevator and exit into a tiny, modest lobby with a hanging silver *Wall Street Journal* logo. I ask the receptionist if I can speak to Sharon Massey. She places a quick call.

"Have a seat and she'll be out in a minute." I sit down on the black couch and began looking over the current edition of the *Journal* sitting on the coffee table in front of me. I had never actually read the paper before. Seeing nothing but business stories perplexes me. I am trying to figure out what kind of paper it is when Sharon comes around the corner. With a friendly smile, she extends her hand. I stand and give her a small stack of photocopies. "I brought you all these—the junk-mail letter, laws, and my ATM slips—so that you can see it all for yourself."

As she stands there shuffling through the papers, I stand in front of her worrying she won't go for it.

"This is a really fun story. I'm going to do it," she announces.

My reply comes out before I can stop it. "Then I won't call the *New York Times* back."

There it is. I have just said something stupid and misleading. I'm shocked by my own desperation. But the remark lands and impacts in a way that I hadn't begun to calculate.

"Don't give the *Times* my story. This is my story! Don't talk to them. I'm just waiting for our lawyers in New York to give me the okay on it. Okay? Promise?" she asks.

It is an easy promise to make. Only an hour before, I was worried the *Wall Street Journal* would reject my story, and now they are afraid to lose it. I go to the window, spread my arms out wide, and soar home. When I land, I call a few friends and tell them they'll be reading my story in the *Wall Street Journal*, any day now.

The Internet

The next day, Thursday, I anxiously want to hear how Sharon's write-up of the story has turned out, but she doesn't call. Friday, several of my friends buy the *Journal* expecting to see my story, but it isn't there. At 3 p.m., I phone Sharon. "She has gone home for the weekend."

I am annoyed.

"What the heck's wrong with this lady, Hobbit? Does she want this story or not? Maybe we will give it to the *Times*!" Hobbit jumps off the desk, flicking his tail, also annoyed.

Monday morning, I call Sharon. She hasn't heard back from New York but she tells me not to worry. "I'll call them this afternoon and get a reply. They should have answered by now." Hobbit sleeps through the call. She never phones back. I go to bed feeling cheated.

Tuesday at noon, I call again. To call so much is unnerving in itself. I know I am risking the perception of my character. I'd like to appear nonchalant and confident, but my desperation is showing.

"Patrick, I was just going to call you. New York approved the story! They like it a lot," she says.

It's a symphony to my ears! My story will run tomorrow. Tomorrow I will have the *Wall Street Journal* on my side!

"I'll call and interview you on Friday."

Her words are like a car crash with my expectations. What is she talking about? Interview me? I already told her the whole story and she liked it. Our first call was the interview.

"What do you mean 'interview me,' Sharon? I already told you the whole story."

"Oh, don't worry, Patrick. I just have to ask you some clarifying questions. That's all."

Her words are reassuring. I'm closer than ever to being in the *Journal*.

"Hobbit, my furry-footed friend, just as sure as you keep trying to lie on the keyboard, I'm going to be in the *Wall Street Journal*!" I kiss his fat, orange face.

Friday arrives, and Sharon phones right on schedule. I have a tape recorder hooked to the phone so that Scott can later hear how the interview went.

"Well, first let me tell that you that I tried to interview someone from First Interstate, but they refused to comment," she begins. "Now, let me ask you, how long was it before you deposited this check that you believed was real?"

With that, my nightmare began.

"Sharon, I didn't think the check was real, and I never said that. I admit I saw the words 'non-negotiable' on it, but..."

"You did?" She cuts in with a voice cold and hard, like steel. "Then why did you deposit it?"

This is no longer the friendly gal I spoke to over the phone or in the lobby. She has been replaced by a reporter, who is my adversary. *I should have called the Enquirer.*

"I deposited it because I thought it would never cash," I reply, trying to keep my cool.

"Then why would you waste your time?"

"It didn't seem like a waste of time to me. It seemed like a joke."

I am desperately hoping my remark puts this line of inquiry to rest.

"So tell me again—*why* did you deposit it?"

Horrifying. I can't believe it. She is convinced I am a criminal. I no longer like this Sharon Massey. She maintains her grilling for an hour. "You weren't trying to defraud the bank?" "Are you afraid the bank will bring criminal charges against you?" "Again, why did you deposit the check?" We might as well be in a small windowless room with a bare lightbulb hanging above my head. Sharon Massey wants me to slip up or finally buckle and shout out my guilt. I want to take back the whole "call a newspaper" idea. But I am forced to repeat the same answers I've already given while trying to hide a rapidly beating chest.

"Did you understand these bank laws before? Is that why you deposited it?"

"Do you think that someone at the bank should get fired for this mistake?"

"Have you been contacted by the FBI or any law enforcement agents?"

"Are you scared that you might go to jail for this?"

"Is this a success strategy you might recommend in your speeches?"

Then, the questions get tougher. She wants to know what I intend to do with the money.

"Sharon, I'm just waiting for a letter from my bank. They said they'd get me one."

"Yes, but what are your intentions—to keep it, or spend it? After all, you say it is legally yours."

"My intention is to wait for the letter from my bank that they told me they'd send."

"Let's say you get it. Then what will you do with the money?"

"Sharon, I'm not trying to avoid your question. I'm trying to stay focused on the more important question of what I'm going to do, and what I'm going to do is wait for a letter from my bank."

I really wish I'd called the Enquirer.

She wraps up the interview with, "Okay, you're not going to tell me, but I'm left to assume that you'd spend money that is legally yours."

"You can assume I'm going to wait for a letter from my bank."

I am drained and sick with a tight double knot in my gut. I try to call Hobbit over from where he is sleeping on a shelf. He flicks his tail hard, which knocks a glass to the floor, where it shatters.

Fuck.

I phone Scott and asked him to come over and listen to the interview as soon as he can. He is convinced that I am exaggerating and says he'll be right over after work. Then I lie down and wish I could die. I want yesterday back. I feel doomed.

Scott arrives and listens to the tape. As he studies every word, his green eyes squint and his right hand massages his beard. "Oh my God, how did you not freak out? Who does she think she works for, *60 Minutes?*"

Smiling, gasping, his eyes wide with excitement, Scott listens to the tape and looks as if he is enjoying his favorite television drama. Only when I speak to him does he mirror my seriousness.

"Total disaster, right? Maybe I can get her to drop the whole story."

"No, no. Don't do that. Maybe we got what we wanted."

"The fucking *Wall Street Journal* is going to print that I'm stealing money! When did we want that?"

"We wanted to keep her guessing about what you intended to do with the money, and you pulled that off—I don't know how, but you did. Of course she wondered if you were good or bad, because we left her hanging."

We? I was the only one on the end of this rope. But maybe he had a point.

"You didn't say anything incriminating, so maybe the story won't make you look bad. And maybe she just had to ask those questions, in case you were a criminal."

Scott's analysis did not alleviate all my doubt. But perhaps it helped a little.

"I asked her if I could see a copy of the story before it ran."

"What did she say?"

"No way."

"That's not a good sign," Scott says, tossing a pen across the desk.

Sharon had told me the article would probably run around the first of August. It seemed like an eternity to wait, but that's all I could do, wait. And check my mail. Sharon had told me to call if I heard anything from my bank. Worrying that the words "They're suing me" or "I'm under arrest" would be the ending to my story kept my stomach firmly in a hard, painful knot.

July 31st

I call Sharon to check in. "Oh, I'm glad you reminded me," she says. "I've still got to write it. Have you heard anything from your bank?"

Glad you reminded me? Still have to write it? WTF?!

I pretend I am not insane with frustration.

Off the phone, I pound my fists loud and fast on the desk and yell. Hobbit leaps up and runs for the hall. "What is she doing, waiting and hoping for me to get sued?"

The next day, Sharon leaves me a message telling me she's written the story and it will run any day now. The relief is immense and almost overwhelming. I was beginning to think the story would never happen. I am determined to have the paper at the first possible moment, so I phone the *Wall Street Journal* for the location and time of the first newspaper drop in my neighborhood. Late that night, I walk ten blocks to the corner of Seventh and Irvine to wait for the midnight delivery. There, in front of the corner drug store, shrouded in thick, cold fog, I find a blue *Wall Street Journal* newspaper box. I sit, pace, and squat for an hour and a half. Finally, at 1:20 a.m., a large blue and yellow delivery truck bearing a *Wall Street Journal* logo pulls up. The driver fills the box not fast enough for my racing nerves. When he pulls away, I move quickly to drop three quarters into the metal slot. They clang to their resting place and free the lid. I pull out a fairly thin paper and search its contents, entirely.

My story isn't there.

My fucking story isn't there.

The next morning, I phone Sharon. I hope with all my might I can restrain myself from lashing out at this woman whom I don't trust.

"It got bumped from the schedule. It happens. I'm not lying to you. I promise it'll run soon. It's a great story. Heard anything from your bank?"

My hope for a friendly story diminishes every time this woman jerks my chain. A lawsuit is going to show up in my mailbox any day now, and perhaps that's exactly what the *Wall Street Journal* is waiting for. I am desperate for a new solution.

A few months earlier, my friend Timothy, a man on the cutting edge of all things computer-related, had introduced me, over pizza, to a nineteen-year-old named Justin Hall. Justin was pioneering a new technology called the World Wide Web. (it would be several more years before it became commonly referred to as the Internet. In 1995, it was still the World Wide Web.)

With long blond hair swept behind his ears and flip-flops on his feet, Justin spoke modestly of his "personal Web page" that was being read by twenty thousand people a day. It took me three slices of pizza to kinda-sorta grasp the concept of the World Wide Web. I'd be lucky if my recently published book was read by more than two thousand people during its lifetime. This guy's stuff was being read by twenty thousand per day? I could barely wrap my head around it. But with the *Wall Street Journal* still not running my story, I remembered Justin's words, "If you ever want to make your own Web page, I'll teach you the required HTML coding in fifteen minutes."

I sat down at my computer on a mission. I feverishly began typing out my check story. It takes me forty-eight hours and twenty pages to tell my story in great detail. Next I seek out young Justin. As he had promised, in fifteen minutes he shows me how to turn my writings into a Web site that I make ready in a matter of days. On August 6, I go back to Justin's apartment.

Justin is standing in the door-frame of a brightly colored Victorian home, dressed in a tie-dyed shirt that stretches almost to his knees. I give him a brief telling of my story.

"Justin, this is your chance to break a story before the *Wall Street Journal* does. What do you say? Will you put a link on your Web page to my story?"

He sweeps his long, straight, blond hair behind his small ears and smiles. "The new media versus the old, eh? Funny, the *Journal*'s where I first read about the Web. Sure," he says with a mellow, peaceful smile. "It's a cool story."

That night his site, Links.net, reads:

"Funny story from my friend Patrick Combs. He got one of those 'You may win $95,000!' sample checks in the mail, and deposited it at his bank. Pretty soon, he looks over his balance, and discovers he is $95,000 richer...www.goodthink.com. Read his story before it appears mangled in next week's *Wall Street Journal*!"

I really found it incomprehensible that twenty thousand people a day could be reading this guy's "Web site," because at the time almost no one had Web sites or knew what they were. But the next morning, I was schooled in the power of the new technology. More than five hundred people read my story on the first night, and e-mails were arriving like a flash flood.

Subject: $95,000 WOW!!!

Subject: What to do?

Subject: Lotsa money from stupid bank.

Subject: the man with the money bags.

Subject: Tell me what I should do!

Subject: About the check.

Subject: What to do

Subject: WHen is a check not a check?

Subject: Heeee Haww!!!!!!

Subject: Keep the loot.

Subject: $95K

Subject: Give it back

Subject: RE: The 95G adventure…

Subject: The Bank Check

Subject: Web page g-think/$$updates.html

Subject: 95.093.35 Adventure

Subject: $100K

Subject: Your cashier's check

Subject: Brilliant, brilliant story!

Subject: what I think you should do…

Subject: Money

Subject: $$,$$$.$$

Subject: great Story!

Subject: The $95,093.35 Question

Subject: The 95,000 solution

Subject: $95K +/-

Subject: Damn you.

Subject: What I think you should do.

Subject: Unbelieveable

Subject: Tell FIB to go fuck themselves!

Subject: Get lawyer/fight!

Subject: The 95,000 man

Subject: The free $95K

I dive in reading in the order they arrived.

Date: Mon, 7 Aug 1995 04:19:16 -0400

To: pcombs@dnai.com

Subject: $95,000 WOW!!!

I just finished reading the detailed account of your expe-
riences with an advertisement check and a highly chagrinned
(though not admittedly) sector of the banking community. I think
that Mr. Persons at FI, in his final conversation with you while
at your mother's house, adopted a new tone with you because he
and his bank most likely talked with their lawyers and found
out that you probably have them by the royal sweets. They are
most likely willing to take the matter as far as criminal charges
in an attempt to scare you into submission or to the point of a
judge telling them that they don't have a case against you. Don't
give in. Keep the money, if not for your own personal financial
gain, but for a muchly deserved lesson to the banking community. If you do, it will make me feel much better about the hundreds of dollars deducted from my own checking account over the
years for NSF fees.

Twenty dollars per bounced check adds up when an average of
three come in before you realize that you forgot to note that $200
ATM cash withdrawal made several weeks earlier.

Good luck with this matter. Your adventure is definitely going to keep me checking your site in the near future.

Respectfully yours,

Tony

GHOST in the MACHINE

Multimedia

Baton Rouge, LA

Date: 7 Aug 95 8:57:19 EDT

To: pcombs@dnai.com

Subject: What to do?

Nice story. Great adventure.

If it was me, and i disregarded the professional concerns you've outlined, I'd give the 95K to charity. However, the professional concerns are legitimate. Hmmm...you've got me puzzled. I don't know...yet. I do know that the bank should not be rewarded for their all too common "I'm-bigger-and-more-powerful-than-you-can-imagine-comply-or-be-driven-into-the-earth-like-a-human-spike" tactics. I'm going to think on this more.

<scott>

From: jdm@europa.com (Drew Barrymore)

Subject: Lotsa money from stupid bank.

To: pcombs@dnai.com

Date: Mon, 7 Aug 1995 08:03:36 -0700 (PDT)

Keep it. It's legally yours. Fascinating story. I definitely learned a lot.

Date: Mon, 7 Aug 1995 11:43:07 -0400 (EDT)

From: Donnan Steele <donnan@minerva.cis.yale.edu>

To: pcombs@dnai.com

Subject: the man with the money bags.

i read through your pages today – you're in an interesting bind with the bank.

breaks and events in life come in all forms. some people inherit money, some people sue for some inane cause and live off the interest forever, some people fall into a good job they're unqualified for, and some people find a tasty half-eaten apple sitting on the subway seat next to them. you take these breaks or leave them behind according to your morals, your feelings on whether you want that event to be a major part of your life.

yours seems to be a fake check.

it's not your money. never was. however, it may legally now be your money. is this how you wanted to make your first 100 grand profit? would you feel good seeing your mom pimping around in that lexus you promised her? it's your decision. write the articles, make jokes about it in your speaches, and ride the wall street wave as far as you can. you should absolutely give the bank as much hell as you can for being bastards to you. is taking $100k of their money as some sort of bizarre fine leveed on them for their cockyness excessive? probably. in the end—money's all the same. greenback dollar bills. -donnan

Date: Mon, 07 Aug 1995 20:09:16 +0100

From: Guy Kewney <guy_kewney@zd.com>

Subject: Tell me what I should do!

To: pcombs@dnai.com

Unfortunately, Netscape threw away the interesting note I sent you; and I can't be assed to re-write it. Summary: it's between you and your conscience if you can persuade the bank to honour that check. But $90K is really a very small amount compared with what you'll earn over the next 20 years, and if it would poison your conscience, then I'd recommend sending it back, with due ceremony.

I've done hoax stories (I'm a writer) and they're great! I still have an award for a totally imaginary software company called SoftCon, which I invented just to prove that ICP awards are commercially purchaseable. Sold the story to a national paper, just like you...

Well done with the hoax!

From: freakboy@owlnet.rice.edu (Shashi Suresh Malkani)
Subject: About the check.
To: pcombs@dnai.com
Date: Mon, 7 Aug 1995 19:24:10 -0500 (CDT)
Dear Mr. Combs,

Assuming your story isn't complete bullshit; we feel that you should cash the check and give the money to the BBC so that they can put "Dr. Who" back in production.
Good Luck!
Shashi Malkani & Greg Bosworth.

Date: Mon, 07 Aug 95 19:41:55 -0700
From: Tony Vollmer <tvollmer@iquest.net>
To: pcombs@dnai.com
Subject: What to do

I don't know if you should keep it. After all, it really isn't yours. However, you should let the bank sit on ice as long as possible! I'd love to be in a position to do that! But, it IS $95,000. That amount would be hard to give back if a court said you could have it. I'm glad I don't have to make that kind of moral disicion! I'll make sure I follow the story! I HAVE to find out whay happens. In any case, GOOD LUCK!

Tony Vollmer

Date: Mon, 07 Aug 95 19:47:59 -0700
From: Glen David Zabriskie <glenzabr@xmission.com>
To: pcombs@dnai.com

Keep the money, the rich bastards deserve it for all the shit they give us all the time.

From: "John C. Ware" <jcw@macromedia.com>
To: pcombs@dnai.com
Subject: (no subject)

Donate the money to charity, report the check stollen from the safe deposit box, and let them squirm.

Just my 2 cents.

Great writing/fun story.

Thanks

--jcw

From: "Steven L. Schnaser" <schna006@maroon.tc.umn.edu>
To: pcombs@dnai.com
Subject: (no subject)

!!!!!!!!!!!!GOOD FOR YOU!!!!!!!!!!!

YOU'VE TAKEN IT THIS FAR MAN, GIT'EM!!!!!!!!!!!!!

From: SamTheButcher <sodaniel@ccnet.com>

To: pcombs@dnai.com

Subject: (no subject)

Try to get NBC to make a movie of the week of it starring Gary Coleman. Or George Clooney. Hold on to the movie rights like you don't need that 95,000 and get a screenwriting credit. Make a cameo as the Bank teller.

You are the American dream, son. I wish I had half the backbone to do what you did.

Sam O'Daniel

From: Tim Kirwin <tkirwin@ix.netcom.com>

To: pcombs@dnai.com

Subject: Give it back

Patrick

I believe you should give the money back. Legally it may be yours, but in the spirit of checks and the "american way of life," the money is not yours.

There must be a way to sell the story without jeopardizing your career.

Tim Kirwin

From: "David A. Milazzo" <damagic@lightspeed.net>

To: pcombs@dnai.com

Subject: (no subject)

Patrick-This is one of the greatest stories I've ever heard! My mother is going to love this. As for your next step? I say fight!!! If the money is legally yours, and from what you have shown it appears to be, then fight for it. I am a First Interstate customer and maybe this will teach them the meaning of the words CUSTOMER SERVICE! Whatever you decide to do, this experience will have a lasting impression on it. Plus, kicking the snot out of one of the largest United States Banking Institutions should feel pretty good too! I'll be watching for the conclusion.

Fondly,

David A. Milazzo

From: rchrd@emf.net
To: pcombs@dnai.com
Subject: WHen is a check not a check?

This is truly an amazing story. Ive never been so glued to my screen online as this!

I think you should play it out to the end. Keep it in your safe box, and insist that you have no intention of spending the money. That flies right in the face of any greed or self gain argument. In the meantime you will drive the banks crazy and maybe stop this sort of sham advertising once and for all.

More power to you. And shame on you for banking with FIB. I left them ten years ago!

Keep me posted.

From: AGiS8@aol.com
To: pcombs@dnai.com

Subject: The Bronze Pig Reminder

Use the money to contract a down-and-out sculpter to create a collasol bronze pig rearing up on its hind legs to revealing an underbelly inscribed with (your, someone's, anyone's) the Ten Commandments of Nice and Honorable Banking. It shouldn't be hard to find someone with the clout to secure an appropriate location for permanent display of this subtle reminder.

From: "Krucke, Carl" <ckrucke@msa.nwschs.sea06.navy.mil>
To: Patrick Combs <pcombs@dnai.com>
Subject: What you could do.
Spend it!

Buy yourself a nice car or something, keep enough for insurance and taxes and all, of course.

Buy all the Jerry Garcia paintings and ties you can find.

Put enough aside for the IRS.

Take the rest, get it into $1 bills. Find a window high above the street across the street from the original bank that took the check. Post on the internet a few days in advance that there will be a give-away. Call the Owen-head bank security guy and tell him about it, about a minute ahead of time, and toss the rest out the window to the appreciative throng below.

Just a suggestion...

Have fun, I'll be watching and pulling for you!

The e-mails are coming in almost faster than I can read them:

"Stick it to the bank because they stick it to us."

"Whenever you feel like you should give it back, just reflect upon how you'd be treated if the error were not in your favor. You'd be steam-rolled for certain."

"Give $1,000 to me. Surely you can remember what it's like to be sixteen and wanting enough money to get a car that girls like."

"You should seriously consider getting a life or some kind of hobby."

"Good luck with this matter. Your adventure is definitely going to keep me checking back for updates."

From: "Michael Sussman" <MSussman@symantec.com>
Message-Id: <9508118108.AA810867872@symantec.com>
To: pcombs@dnai.com
Subject: $95,000
Patrick -

This is one terrific story. I won't suggest what you should do, as I don't know what I'd do. However, I am reminded of this joke:

A heart surgeon explains to his patient that he needs a transplant immediately. Fortunately, there are TWO compatible hearts available at that time. One heart had belonged to a 25-year-old athlete who didn't smoke or drink and was never sick. The athlete died in a car accident. The second heart belonged to a banker who enjoyed rich food, liquor, and cigars.

The banker died of old age.

Surgeon: Which heart would you like to have?

Patient: I'm sure I want the banker's heart.

Surgeon: The banker's heart! Why?

Patient: Because I want a heart that's never been used!

Anyway, Patrick, enjoy the ride.

Michael Sussman

I am howling at my desk with laughter. Then I read one more e-mail.

From: Randall Friedman <randman@direct.ca>

To: pcombs@dnai.com

Subject: What to do.

I congratulate you on your ingenuity and It's hard to know what I would do unless I was actually in your position. some thoughts Banks have always been completly unconcerned as to their customers circumstances when it comes to outrageous service charges and using their powerful legal representation to use the letter of the law to acquire as much property and money and power as possible. After all profit is the bottom line for most corperate institutions.

TV Nation (on fox) last evening, did an expose on outrageous bank charges in their Corporate Crime segment: The banks are constantly changing charges (no set rate) and purposly manipulate the way they process cheques and deposits (they process the cheques before the deposites and that they cash the largest cheques first so that if you over draw then you will have more, smaller cheques that they can charge you for) they quoted statistical figure in the billions of dollars in profit every year from NSF. charges alone.

If you deal with them on the same grounds inwhich they deal with every other customer that they have then you will work to keep the money.

If you are having trouble or will have trouble dealing with your feelings later then maybe you can make a win win solution of giving some of the money back and keeping an amount for your hardship and a reward for being so astute.

I would also seriously considering a large amount of money for giving an exclusive story to any paper, after all the news papers are in the business to make money and people will want to read your story. I hope that you are working on a plan so that you will be able to take advantage of the popularity and fleeting fame you might incure in the near future.

Like the boyscouts of America say Be prepared, get a good lawyer you can trust, and market and promote,promote,promote. Many have said there is no such thing as good or bad publicity just publicity, its what you do with it that will determine the outcome.

Thanks for the opportunity to participate, good luck, ill be checking back to see what happens.

If you every need genuine advice on stereo or audio equipment give me a call, I have been designing home theater systems for the last 15 yrs. ;-}

I am encouraged. My story is perfect *Wall Street Journal* material. I phone Sharon and push her to run my story or let me give it to the *Times*. "It's on the launch pad. I can't tell you when—it's policy—and I can't even tell you 'it' means your story," she says like an informant. "But if I were you, I'd wake up in the morning and buy the *Wall Street Journal*."

On went the album *Tim* by The Replacements, loud.
I am going to be in the news! Owen Persons would soon
be typing me an apology letter at two hundred words per
minute. And maybe, just maybe, because of the publicity, I will be able to get the bank to give all the money
to charity.

THE WAITING

That night, I wait again anxiously for the delivery truck in the fog and darkness, only to find nothing of my story. Nothing the next night either. Scott comments, "Maybe this is the *Wall Street Journal*'s way of getting us to buy their paper."

"I'm doing everything I can to get it on the schedule as soon as possible. Give me till Tuesday or Wednesday, please," Sharon tells me, trying to ease my anger.

On Tuesday, I don't go wait at the paper box, and don't find my story when I check in the morning. On Wednesday, I also sleep instead of standing out in the cold. Around 9 a.m., in go my coins and out comes the brand new edition. My eyes search frantically, as my hands flip the pages, only to find a story about the first summer camp to have e-mail capability. Furiously, I crumple the pages into the trashcan attached to the lamp post. Then I kick, kick, kick the hard, plastic container until my anger dissipates to disappointment. They are never going to run my story.

Sharon sounds as defeated as I feel. "New York killed the story. I'm so pissed. I understand your giving it to someone else who will run it. I'll keep trying, but there's not much more I can do."

I put in calls to *USA Today* and the *New York Times*, but neither returns my call. My news chances are over. I am a fool for having believed it was a story for the big papers, and I can feel it like an anvil lodged in my stomach. I will now have to call my friends and say, "Forget about it. It's not going to be in any paper. No biggie." They'll be embarrassed for me. Two thousand people are checking my Web site daily for story updates also. They too are waiting on the *Journal* article because I've promised them it's coming. Many think the whole story is fiction. The write-up was going to be my proof. The lack of a *Wall Street Journal* story is going to make me look like a liar.

Besides e-mail, snail mail is the only thing left I have to check daily. Every day, I check my black metal mailbox, hoping not to find a letter from my bank, but one day I do. A cream-colored, standard-sized envelope with the orange and black First Interstate logo is lurking behind my phone bill. I sit down on the bottom step of the stoop and open the letter, dreading the threatening and accusatory letter I am sure to find. It is a single page on linen stationery, tri-folded. My fingers are already damp as I begin to read.

Dear Patrick Combs:

We would like to thank you for maintaining your account here at First Interstate Bank of California. We sincerely appreciate the opportunity to serve you. I trust that we are providing the services you need and adding to your financial security as well.

To express our appreciation, we have arranged to provide a new benefit for all eligible checking account customers—$1,000 of Accidental Death and Dismemberment Insurance. There is NO COST to you at any time. We pay the premiums.

Sincerely,

Michael A. Johnson, Senior Vice President

Dismemberment? I wonder which member they cut off first?

I laugh myself into the house over the form letter. Mr. Johnson is seriously out of the loop about my account, or seriously evil. Maybe I will write him back. Maybe just, "Dear Mr. Johnson, Are you threatening me?"

Later that afternoon, I receive a phone call from a Hollywood producer. He has read my Web pages and is interested in my check story as a movie. "But I need to see how it ends. Whether you get to keep the money or you go to jail, from our point of view, both make for a good ending. And, if you do go to jail, we won't have to pay for the rights to the story—just a point of fact." End of call.

"Hobbit, I need to decide what to do next," I say, scratching him behind his ears. He is purring loudly, feeling good enough to drool. It seems like my options are to call the bank or not call the bank. Calling them would require another attempt to get them to send me a letter that officially requested the money back. Been there, done that. Not calling them potentially allowed them to forget about the whole thing and write off the money as a small loss, as one of my friends said banks do at the end of every year. I don't see myself calling them. I am either going to get sued or keep the money and decide what to do with it later. Hobbit rolls onto his side to have his belly rubbed.

The next day, August 15, I receive a voice mail. "The story is scheduled to run tomorrow. I won't promise since you know how that's gone, but it is on the schedule." It is Sharon's perfectly familiar voice. I'd heard it a million times before and would be a fool to believe it again. But I want so much for it to be true. Her voice seems different this time—slower and more measured. Maybe that means something. I really want it to. The prospect of the story being a disparaging article seems less since Sharon's voice is friendly. I really want my story in the *Wall Street Journal*.

At midnight, I am standing yet again by the newspaper box, waiting for an hour, trying not to get my hopes up. The now familiar driver and I exchange hellos—I figure he takes me for an insomniac or a hyperdriven stock broker. I wait for him to pull away and then do exactly as I have done so many times before. Three coins in, one paper out. I spread the paper across the top of the blue *Wall Street Journal* box and begin flipping black and white pages. Nothing on the front or in its inside sections. Fooled again, I think, flipping angrily, until I see the words, *"Prankster Exploits a Bank's Gaffe And Turns Trash Into Quick Cash."*

By Sharon Massey, Staff Reporter of The Wall Street Journal

"Patrick Combs recently performed an experiment that any medieval alchemist would aspire to: He turned a piece of junk mail into cold, hard cash."

THE WALL STREET JOURNAL

MARKETPLACE

Prankster Exploits a Bank's Gaffe And Turns Trash Into Quick Cash

By SHARON MASSEY
Staff Reporter of THE WALL STREET JOURNAL.

Patrick Combs recently performed an experiment that any medieval alchemist would aspire to: He turned a piece of junk mail into cold, hard cash.

The only problem is, he performed the experiment on a bank, and the bank wants its money back.

Mr. Combs, a 29-year-old San Francisco author, was one of 40 million Americans who recently received a fake check in the mail as part of a promotional campaign by the Association of Certified Liquidators, a company that buys and resells stores' unsold goods.

Unlike the other recipients, however, Mr. Combs deposited the $95,093.35 "check" in his account at Los Angeles-based First Interstate Bancorp, as a lark. He just wanted to see what would happen, he says.

"I was absolutely certain the bank wouldn't cash it," says Mr. Combs.

But lo and behold, the bank credited the entire sum to his account by May 22, the next business day.

Mr. Combs waited three weeks, expecting the bank to discover its error. When it didn't, he withdrew every last penny and put a cashier's check for the full amount in

his safe-deposit box at the bank — and he has a deposit slip and copy of the cashier's check to prove it.

"There's no way I'd leave the bank with that much money," he says. "If fate can give it to me, it can take it away just as fast."

The bank now hopes to do just that. A week after he withdrew the money, Mr. Combs discovered — when an automated teller machine ate his bank card — that his account had been frozen, he says. He also received what he describes as threatening messages on his home answering-machine from bank representatives ordering him to give back the loot. Mr. Combs refused. He says he would have returned the money if the bank had been more polite.

"I would have liked the bank to just call me and admit it erred," says Mr. Combs. "And maybe take me to lunch."

First Interstate, citing customer confidentiality, declines to comment on the case.

ACL President Mitch Klass is surprised by the financial uproar caused by his company's errant check.

"No one has ever tried to cash one of our promotional checks before," he says. "I didn't even know it this time. We're going to have to check into this."

It is a fun article, not a fraud article. I run with the newspaper in hand more than a mile, to Scott's house, whooping along the way. I let myself in with the key he has under a porch plant and burst in on him sleeping.

"We did it, man! We got our article in the *Wall Street Journal*!"

Scott jerks to a sitting position. "Holy shit! If I kept a gun by the bed, I'd have shot you."

"Listen. *Combs recently performed an experiment that any medieval alchemist would aspire to: He turned a piece of junk mail into cold, hard cash. The only problem is, he performed the experiment on a bank, and the bank wants its money back. Mr. Combs was one of 40 million Americans who recently received a fake check.* Forty million! I bet I'm not the only one who deposited it, just the only one who told."

"It goes on to summarize the story and then says I deposited it on *a lark*. I like that. Listen, it quotes me. *I would have liked the bank to just call me and admit it erred, and maybe take me to lunch.* And listen to this: *First Interstate, citing customer confidentiality, declines to comment on the case. ACL President Mitch Klass is surprised by the financial uproar caused by his company's errant check. "No one has ever tried to cash one of our promotional checks before," he says. "I didn't even know it had happened. We're going to have to check into this."* No pun intended. What a liar. I called and told him!"

"It doesn't say a word about my intentions on what to do next. There's only a sentence that says...*Bank representatives ordered him to give back the loot. Mr. Combs refused.*

He says he would have returned the money if the bank had been more polite. So true. Scott, what the hell do you think?"

Scott's sleepy expression has turned to absolute delight.

"This is perfect! Just enough to make you really want to know how it's going to end. People are going to eat this shit up!"

I run through the dark and empty streets of San Francisco, shouting, dancing, and pumping my fists toward the few stars that can be seen through the orange street lights. At home, I blast the stereo, post the great news to my Web site, and read the story over and over till 6 a.m.

I sleep until noon and only get out of bed because the phone keeps ringing. On my voice mail, I find fourteen messages. I sit at my desk in my underwear listening to them all. The first is from a man with a thick New York accent. "Yo, I'm sitting at my breakfast table laughing my ass off. Mother of God. Thanks for making my day. Keep da money." Click. This unknown Joe Blow outs-cooped every news agency in the country, but didn't so much as leave his name.

"This is KGO news radio…"

"I'm from the Associated Press…"

"Patrick, I'm with Channel 4 news…"

"I'm a producer at the *David Letterman Show*…"

"We'd love to have you on the *Tonight Show with Jay Leno*…"

The rest are radio shows. It is a response beyond my wildest dreams. Letterman, Leno, and the Associated Press make the top of my callback list.

The reporter from the Associated Press wire interviews me by phone and says she'll write the story that afternoon. She loves what I told her and doesn't ask twice about what I intend to do with the money or why I made the deposit in the first place. At the end she says, "I suggest you refrain from doing any more interviews for the day. That way your story stays fresh and has a greater chance of being sent out on our national wire."

I take her advice and phone no one else back, except Letterman and Leno. Both producers have me tell them the story in my own words. Both express interest in having me on their shows as soon as their hiatus ends in two weeks. "If the *Tonight Show* contacts you, you'll have to choose between us, and you should choose us," says Letterman's producer. "If you want to be on with Jay, you can't say yes to those guys," says the producer of the *Tonight Show*.

Next, I prepare for an all-day leadership workshop I am facilitating at Arizona State University the next day. It is my first scheduled speech of the new school year and the first I've had since May when school ended. It is hard to stay focused on my work. My mind is on the media, and my bank's reaction. But now I feel safe. I have stepped out from a dark alley and onto a well-lit street.

Fifteen Minutes of Fame

By 6:00 the next morning, twenty-five new messages flash on my voice mail. I can only listen to a few of them before rushing out the door for a Super Shuttle to the airport.

"Patrick, this is Kim, with America's Talking Network..."

"Hi, this is Hurricane Stevens down in Baton Rouge. I'm sure a lot of other morning DJs are trying to reach you, but call us back first, okay—you're our hero..."

"Hi, Art Bell with the CBC radio network. I broadcast a little show out of Nevada..."

All the new calls mean that the Associated Press story did go out on the national wire. As a matter of fact, it went out on the international news wire.

I board my flight and sit down next to a man in a spotted yellow tie. Shortly after takeoff, he asks me where I am headed to. It doesn't matter what he asked me because I would have taken any question and turned it into an opportunity to announce my good fortune. "I'm going to speak at Arizona State, but it's one of the craziest days of my life. You see..." I am the seatmate that won't shut up. When I get to the part about the branch manager telling me the money was mine, a man wearing a blue-striped tie leans my way across the aisle and says, "You're the guy that cashed the check? Let me shake your hand. I read the story in the *Wall Street Journal*, and I was just reading another story about you in today's *San Jose Mercury News*." My face heats up like an oven coil as he holds up his newspaper and points to the large headline: *Man 1, Bank 0*.

At ASU, thirty engineering students attend my workshop in a beige conference room with seating in the shape of a U. I speak four hours about leadership when all I really want to talk about is the junk-mail check. Regrettably, I cannot think of a way to relate my windfall good fortune to leadership.

When the workshop is over, I race to check my voice mail. Forty-eight messages!

"This is Robin from Paramount Pictures..."

"Patrick, we love what you did! Call us, Marshall and Maxell in Baltimore..."

"George from *NBC Nightly News* with Tom Brokaw..."

"Johnny Dare and Murphy from KQRC in Kansas City. Great job, Patrick! Can you tell us where to get one of those checks?"

"Gary calling from *Hard Copy*..."

"Hi, Annie from *ABC News* with Peter Jennings and Diane Sawyer..."

"Hello, Bonnie from CNN..."

"Hi, this is Felicia from the *Montel Williams Show*..."

"John-Michele with *Current Affair*"

"Patrick, our hero, this is Paul with Froggie 99. Call us first, buddy. We love what you did."

"Hi, this is Debbie with the *Leeza Show*..."

"Jay Diamond with ABC radio."

"I'm with the *Late Late Show with Greg Kinnear*."

"My name is Jamie. I'm a producer with *Dateline NBC*..."

"This is Mindy with *Good Morning America*..."

"Donna with *Day and Date* on CBS..."

"Karen with CNBC's *The Money Club*."

"Hi, Patrick, Sandy from Channel 7. We remember when you delivered the baby."

"I'm calling from the Jim Bohannon show. Jim would love to have you on..."

"Graham with BBC radio in London."

"Susie from the *Phil Donahue Show*."

The messages go on and on. They are from news channels and seemingly every morning radio show in the country. I drop the hotel phone back into its cradle and launch into rapid pacing between the window and door or up and over the hotel bed. It isn't enough to deal with all the bursting energy that tingles my skin, so I run out the door and down a random path through the hotel hallway. I come to a large window that overlooks buildings, homes, palms, golf courses, and dry flats. The green courses in the desert appear as unreal as my world feels. I feel both excited and overwhelmed. It is already past 5 p.m. I will begin returning calls tomorrow morning.

Up at six, I phone all the TV news channels first, hoping the airtime would further ward off an attack from my bank. "I'll be back in San Francisco at 1:30 p.m.," I tell each. "We'll meet you at your home and interview you this afternoon," they reply.

As I pull up in a taxi, I see four camera crews waiting near the steps of my apartment. They have formed a line based on who arrived first. Channel 4 News, Channel 7, Channel 2, and *NBC Nightly News.*

One at a time, each respective crew, made up of a reporter, cameraman, and sound guy, comes in and transforms my office into a suitable place to do an interview. They set up lights, tape paper over the windows, hang microphones, and point cameras. They come in hoping for a fun story, and get a one-man show. Animated like a chimp, with gestures big enough for Carnegie Hall, I reenact the initial wow of my $95,000 bank balance, and the threatening anger of Owen Persons. Like an overly dramatic guest on a daytime talk show, I gleefully entertain with lines such as, "I would have returned the money if they hadn't acted so mean" and "Banks seem to have forgotten that treating customers well still matters." I am swept up in my fifteen minutes. They are swept away by the fantasy.

"Patrick, what are you going to do now?" asks each smiling reporter.

"My ideal outcome would be for the president of the bank to call me and say, 'Let's go to lunch.' We'd work it out in a fair, decent, and honest way. Maybe give all the money to charity." It is an answer I'd thought a lot about. A perfect ending. The president and I dining on caesar salad and sparkling water at a table decorated with a single red orchid, sharing a laugh, shaking hands, and then standing to present a giant light-green check to a smiling and grateful, smartly dressed man or woman from the Association Against Junk Mail. The whole thing captured on camera. "Bank takes a joke and turns it into $95,000 of charity. Full story at eleven."

While the NBC news crew sits down to join me for dinner, *Good Morning America* calls and arranges for me to fly out to New York for an appearance.

The very next day, I am in New York, delivered there by limo, sitting under the bright lights of the ABC studio doing a three-minute chat with Charlie Gibson. It's clear he doesn't like me a much at all. He acts a bit stand-offish as he questions me, and he uses the F word. "Is this fraud?" he asks, with a wide-eyed smile. I laugh it off, and he keeps it light from there on, but I feel a look of accusation in his eyes.

That evening, my story airs on both NBC and ABC nightly news. I catch the ABC segment in a crowded airport bar. I watch a re-enactment of myself checking my mailbox and making a deposit at an automatic bank machine. Then I tell my story with gestures befitting a person on speed. It came across, I think, as pretty funny. The segment closes with my appeal to the president for lunch. Diane Sawyer, from behind her news desk, caps it with a deadpan, "I wouldn't count on that lunch, Patrick."

My story also appears in more than two hundred newspapers that week, including the *New York Times*.

The next two weeks finds me on the road giving college speeches scheduled in Missouri, Ohio, Tennessee, Illinois, New York, Virginia, and Kentucky. Around every presentation, I jam in phone interviews. Ten days into touring, exhausted, I phone Scott from a hotel room in Fairfax, Virginia.

He says, "Everybody's talking about your story. I was standing next to people at Tivoli's yesterday who were talking about it."

"I can't tell you how many people I run into who know about it. I was sitting next to a lady on my plane who recognized me. A cabby a couple days ago brought it up without knowing it was me. I didn't let on so I could hear his take on it. He thought it was great."

"It is! I saw you on *Montel*. It was hilarious to see the audience break into applause. I like your line about not letting fear win—that was pretty cool, actually."

"It's all pretty crazy," I say, falling back onto the hotel bed and kicking off my shoes.

"How are you holding up? How are your speeches going?"

"I spoke to six hundred freshman at George Mason University today. It was excellent. Yesterday, a live satellite broadcast of my talk from the University of Tennessee went to sixty schools. Awesome. And in between, I'm either flying or doing radio interviews from morning to midnight. I've done over fifty. And get this—*Hard Copy* flew a crew to my hotel today and taped an interview."

"Oh my God! That show is so lame. Are you sure you want to be on that?"

"Too late now. I think it's gonna be funny."

"Do you get paid for these interviews?" Scott asks through the phone.

"*Hard Copy* tells you that they don't pay for interviews because they're journalists, but that they do pay for any source materials you might have, wink wink, nudge nudge. They agreed to pay me $1,000 for the right to film my copy of the cashier's check."

"That is so damn funny."

"But that's the only show that has offered me any money."

I pick up the remote and aim it at the TV. It flickered on.

"Are you going to be on Letterman or Leno?"

"I don't think either. They were both on a week's vacation when they called, and now they think they missed the right timing."

"What are they talking about?" Scott practically yells. "Did you know you're in *Entertainment Weekly* right now as the number two thing people in the country are talking about?"

"What?"

"Yeah, dude. You're listed in their *Hot Sheet* column, second only to something about the Queen."

"No kidding?"

"Yeah. And you're above Microsoft paying millions for the right to use the Rolling Stones song "Start Me Up" to launch Windows 95."

I click past 10 o'clock news shows. "*Dateline NBC* did a feature story on sweepstakes checks last night."

"Did they mention you?"

"I don't know. I didn't see it."

"I can't believe all this."

"Yeah, it's unreal."

"Any word from your bank yet?"

"Nothing. Supposedly they even turned down a call from Diane Sawyer."

"What are they thinking?! They're so stupid. They could turn this into free positive publicity."

"I completely agree. I have no idea what they're thinking, but you can bet they're pissed."

"Are you worried about it?"

"Yeah, truthfully I am. Lately I've been thinking that my bank has decided to wait until all this publicity blows over, and *then* hit me with everything they've got. Whether they know it or not, keeping quiet through this whole thing is very intimidating. It makes them seem even meaner."

When the call is over, I plug the hotel phone cord into the back of my Mac laptop and log on for my e-mail. In pour over a hundred e-mails. I sit up another ninety minutes reading them all. It has become a nightly routine that engrosses me. The vast majority always express support, but every batch is a mixed bag.

"Keep it. You did nothing wrong. If someone jokingly offers to pay their restaurant tab with seashells and the restaurant accepts them, does that make the diner a fraud or the restaurateur stupid?"

"I caught your cheque story on UK Channel 4 news. I was gob-smacked!"

"Give all the money to charity—you'll be a hero."

"It was wrong of you to deposit the check in the first place, so give the money back."

"Spend it on liquor and prostitutes!!!!! And don't forget, you're on Al Gore's information superhighway!"

"It's not your money just because the bank made mistakes."

"Look into the bank fraud provisions (forgot the code section) of Title 18, United States Code. What you did could get you up to 30 years in prison."

"Use the money to lobby for a law to protect senior citizens against junk-mail checks."

"Practice random acts of banking and senseless deposits!"

"You suck…Your story isn't that amazing."

"I notice your e-mail address is at dnai.com. Obviously it stands for Does Not Allow Intimidation."

"You may be interested to know that you made the New Zealand national TV news last night."

"Here's a synopsis that's a good deal less self-serving than your account: an idiot receives an advertisement that looks like a check, the idiot deposits the advertisement, the only 'explanation' the idiot offers is that he thought it would NEVER clear. This is frankly not credible, and the fact that the idiot does not allow the funds to be immediately returned to the rightful owner casts further doubt on it."

"A similar thing happened to my wife and I. We spent some of the money and the bank charged us with bank robbery! We've been fighting the charges for a year now. Smart you didn't spent the money."

"I bet you anything the bank took back their cashier's check a long time ago without even telling you. I bet you've got nothing sitting in your safe deposit box, dumb ass. It would explain why you haven't heard from them."

And then I click on this email:

From: Chris Ellinger <heywally@SIRIUS.COM>
Date: 31, Aug 95 08:41:24 0700
To: pcombs@dnai.com
Subject: (no subject)
Hey!

I'm a teller at the FI branch in Mill Valley. We got a memo last week saying we should keep our mouths shut about the situation.

A lot of people are really uptight about this and very little joking is tolerated.

Good luck to you and I hope you get what you asked for!

WALLY!

I dash off an e-mail back to Wally.

From: pcombs@.dnai.com (Patrick Combs)

Date: 31, Aug 1995 19:32:49 -0700

To: Chris Ellinger <heywally@SIRIUS.COM>

Subject: Re: (no subject)

Wally,

What would it take for me to receive a copy of this memo mailed to home (anonymously, of course)?? I would post the memo to my Web page (not ever mentioning, naming, remembering, or even knowing who sent it to me). The entertainment value of letting folks read it would be an absolute SCREAM! It would be the first glimpse of FICAL's true reaction to this situation.

Please, Please! Please!!

My address is

Patrick Combs

326 Carl Street

San Francisco, CA 94117

What do you say?

I fold up my computer and call to check my answering machine back home. One message. It's a man I don't know:

"You're holding up a major merger. It can't go forward until First Interstate gets this egg off their face. From a supporter on the inside who must remain anonymous."

Click. No traceable info.

I am bewildered. I click off the bedside lamp. Once again I'll get only four hours sleep before heading off to another airport. I lay awake a long time, too tired to sleep. Was I really holding up a merger? Was my cashier's check still in the safe deposit box? I'd look when I returned home. What if I really gave all the money to charity? Did I have the right? I drift to sleep with too many thoughts on my mind.

NOT GUILTY

On Friday, September 1, I return home from my speaking tour. A reader of my Web page has mailed me a bottle of wine. I also receive two *Late Show with David Letterman* baseball caps his producers had sent before they had decided not to have me on. My homecoming coincides with my *Hard Copy* air date. I plug a videotape into the VCR and sit down on the couch to watch. *Hard Copy* sounds like it's scripted by Dr. Seuss. "He deposited it for yuks not bucks!...The bank made a gargantuan, Godzilla-sized goof-up."

Hard Copy does a great job with the story. It is the only show that includes mention of the laws that are in my favor. The segment ends with a phone-in poll that asks viewers, *"What do you think Patrick should do with the money?"*

A total of 7,542 people paid one dollar each to vote I should keep it; 2,043 people paid to say I should give it back; and 1,013 people paid good money to vote, "I don't know." Only in America.

I am replaying the segment when the doorbell rings.

Every time the doorbell has rung during the past two months, I have worried that it might be a court server with legal documents. At the bottom of the stairs stands a thin, plainly dressed man my age holding papers.

"Patrick Combs? I saw you on TV last week and I want to tell you that I support what you're doing. I don't know if you know this, but you're a hero to me and all my friends. We're rooting for you to keep the money and stick it to the man for all of us."

"Thanks, man, I'll try."

"But unfortunately, I also have to make a living, so... Patrick Combs, you've just been served. Sorry."

I sign where he points. He hands me a manila envelope, as thick and heavy as a double issue of a women's fashion magazine, but not as heavy as the feeling in my body.

"Just gotta make a living. I *do* hope you win."

His sincerity, although ironic, eases the tension in my neck. "Thanks, that means a lot."

I slog up to my apartment, collapse onto the couch, and slide out the white papers. I dread seeing the words *fraud, felony, stolen funds, criminal mischief*, and possibly even *bank robbery*. Weak feelings pour through me like molasses. I have never been in legal trouble before. These papers could start a battle that could destroy my reputation. A court case could also devour money I didn't have. I begin reading, and brace myself for the worst. But page after page, the words I dread are nowhere to be found. No fraud charges. No robbery. No criminal mischief. The papers merely set a court appearance and plead for a judgment that restricts me from cashing the cashier's check. A different court appearance would be pursued later to decide the money's rightful owner, the papers say. They repeatedly mention my bank balance (negative one hundred and seventy five dollars) to point out the near impossibility of recovering spent money from a motivational speaker so poor. It feels like they have nothing real to hit me with, and that I am in the driver's seat.

The documents I had expected to make me cry actually made me laugh a bit. First Interstate Bank of California was abbreviated throughout as FICAL. An acronym I pronounce as "fecal," not "fical." So these are my fecal matters.

With only one week until my court date, I have to decide what to do. I'm hoping I can find my answer in the day's batch of e-mail. Among the usual parade of mostly praising e-mails, one stands out:

Date: 1, Sept 1995 15:31:01 U

From: "Connolly Mike" <connolly_mike@bah.com>

Subject: Re: $95K--BBS postings

To: "Patrick Combs" <pcombs@dnai.com>

Back about twenty years ago in Chicago, some auto dealership printed a coupon in the local newspapers saying that if you bought a car from them and brought in the coupon, they would knock $500 off the cost of the car. They failed to limit one per customer.

As a result, one woman collected enough coupons from the neighbors' papers and her own purchases to buy the most expensive car on the lot and pay for it with newspaper clippings. And you know what the courts found? Vendor emptor: the car was hers because the dealership failed to anticipate where their incompetence could lead."

Gotta go, there's a personal letter from Ed McMahon to ME, telling me I may have already WON!

Although the e-mail suggests that I have a legitimate shot at winning in court, I do not like the story. I read it and know that I don't want to be like the Chicago woman, taking advantage of a loophole, and yet my bank is painting me into a corner. Could FICAL be any stupider, preferring to go to court rather than give me a simple letter? It pisses me off.

The legal document has a name and number for FICAL's senior counsel, Mr. Bernard Meyers, so I go to my desk and call him. I am determined to get my letter. Meyers answers and knows exactly who I am.

"Mr. Meyers, I don't know what you've been told about me or what your impressions are, but I'm an easy guy to talk to. Would you like to give the old-fashioned way of resolution a chance? Will you meet me to discuss this matter?"

"I'd love to."

"Good. How about tomorrow?"

"Tomorrow at my office, say one o'clock. How's that?"

"Excellent."

"I'll see you there."

"Mr. Meyers, one quick question."

"Yes?"

"Did you see me on TV saying I'd give back the money in exchange for a simple letter?"

"I don't watch much TV, Patrick. But maybe you'll tell me more about that letter tomorrow."

I can't help but doubt that he hasn't seen me on TV.

Mr. Meyers works on the twenty-fifth floor of a skyscraper owned by First Interstate. As much as the sensible part of my brain knows that I am perfectly safe walking into my bank's building, another part of me feels like a fugitive entering an FBI office on a promise of temporary immunity. I enter the building chanting to myself, *Today, I'll clean up this fecal matter.*

I exit the elevator, check in at the lobby desk, and soon meet Mr. Bernard Meyers. Our meeting is a poker game from the minute I walk in. I see him quickly size me up, with my jeans and white-collar business shirt. His crisp white shirt and dollar-green suspenders seem to be custom fit for his barrel chest. He is balding but fit, and wears wire-frame glasses that make him look smart but friendly. He invites me into a small conference room and offers me a cup of coffee or tea. I accept the tea.

He smiles while he asks me if I prefer milk, sugar, or honey. His movements give no nervousness away. But as he prepares my tea, I catch him looking at me in brief stares of scrutiny and suspicion. Then we get down to business, sitting across the conference table from one another. I take charge with an explanation of my experience. He listens with complete presence and no emotion. Nothing I say is impacting him, apparently. He seems neither surprised nor impressed. His confidence suggests that he holds the winning cards, despite what I am saying.

But then I see it. When I begin detailing the laws in my favor and hand him photocopies, Mr. Meyer's cheeks twitch—both of them—like Jell-O, jiggling for only an instant. It is a twinge of anger. He instantly covers it with a smile, but it is too late.

"Mr. Meyers, all this bank needs to do to get the money back from me is give me the letter I asked for at the start."

"What kind of letter?"

"All I'm asking for is a letter that states the truth of how this matter unfolded. That way, if, in a future job interview—say at a bank—I was asked, 'Say, aren't you the guy who tried to bilk a bank for $95,000?' I could present them with the letter and clear up the wrong impression."

"Assuming they'd want to hire you otherwise," Mr. Meyers responds, spoken as a normal clarification, with a dash of sarcasm.

"It needs to detail how we got to this point—all the mistakes involved, my attempts to cooperate."

Bernard begins taking notes on his yellow legal pad.

"And it needs to have legal assurances that will safeguard me from any future legal action by the bank."

"Our only interest is in the return of the cashier's check. We won't pursue any legal action if you return it."

"I believe you, Mr. Meyers, but I'd need it in the letter just in case you change jobs a year from now and someone else wants to be unreasonable."

Bernard makes the note. "I can produce a letter for you, Patrick, and hopefully we can resolve this without wasting your time and money in court."

"Excellent, Mr. Meyers," I reply.

Bernard forces a rapid and shallow smile onto his face, then looks down to begin another note to himself. "And we assume you'll be closing your account."

No you didn't just say that.

"No, I wasn't planning on doing that," I reply.

Bernard looks at me as if I hadn't heard him.

"Does First Interstate want me to close my account?" I ask, quite stunned.

"First Interstate isn't *asking* you to close your account, but it would *please* First Interstate if you would," he says carefully.

Unf---inbelievable.

I leave Mr. Meyers office, happy to have the end in sight, thinking the bank will simply deliver the letter soon and this whole thing will be behind me.

The next day, there is a letter in my box, in a First Interstate envelope. Two sheets of paper. The first is lined paper and hand scrawled at high speed.

"Hey PAtrick!

It Should make a lovely Souvenier!

Viva La Revolucion!

Wally

PPS - Eat this Note!!"

The second page is a First Interstate memo on pink paper.

"Bank Security Department

WARNING

For internal use only.

Non-Negotiable Instruments.

Attention tellers and employees who accept customer transactions."

The memo educates tellers on how to spot a check marked "Non-negotiable." "Employees are advised that these items are non-negotiable and not to be accepted under any circumstances." Alone in my room, I am laughing my ass off. Long live Wally!

October 1, 1995

Little did I know when I walked out of Mr. Meyers' office on September 2 that I had a month of shitty letters and cold telephone negotiations still ahead of me. In the first four drafts of the letter, First Interstate could only produce blame and lies. Then, adding insult to injury, Meyers sent me a letter stating I must pay $266 to cover what it cost to file their lawsuit in court. "Not in a million," I said. They let it go.

I was deep into thinking I may never get the letter I was requesting, but then my fax machine rang, and out poured another legal letter from FICAL. It was all there: a detailed account of First Interstate's banking errors, letters of apology sent by First Interstate to those who received bounced checks because of my frozen account, proof that my credit rating was undamaged, a complete dismissal of all charges and damage claims, and the right to continue speaking and writing about the experience. Many had told me the bank would never meet all my demands. It just had. It doubled as a settlement agreement we would both sign. The bottom of the first paragraph had the words I was really looking for:

"**FICAL** made an error."
Four words.
Four words.
That night, over dinner with Scott and a few other friends, the question comes up whether I'd ever thought of giving all the money to charity. This was, for me, ethically the slipperiest slope of all. I'd spent many, many nights reveling in the idea of giving it all to charity. And a continual stream of e-mails cheering for me

to "give it to charity" and "stick it to the bank" let me know it would clearly be a very popular move. But as the whole escapade progressed, I realized that I didn't want to "stick it" to anyone. I merely wanted to stand up for myself. And giving the money to the poor was not the way to right the bank's wrongs, because deep down I didn't feel the money was ethically mine to give. Don't get me wrong; the bank could go F themselves as far as I was concerned for their bad behavior. But when I thought through the fantasy of robbing from the rich to give to the poor, I concluded that Robin Hood was kind of an asshole. Nobody at the dinner table really agreed.

October 3rd

Most reporters had told me to call again with updates. I phone the woman at the Associated Press. She interviews me about my decision to give back the money and later sends the story out to the wire. My meeting with Mr. Meyers to sign the agreement and return the money is set for tomorrow, Tuesday, October 4, at 1:30 p.m. He told me to come straight to his office.

There are a few messages on my machine from news agencies that hope to meet me at the bank for interviews and footage. I return their calls and invite them.

I go to sleep fully intending to give back the money the next day. But that night, at 3:22 a.m., I sit straight up having a very lucid dream. I will take the cash to Vegas and bet it all at 49/51 odds on the roulette wheel. If I win, I'll have $95,000 to do with as I please and $95,000 to give back to the bank! It will be such an audacious move that every news agency who's somebody will show up to cover it. Now, if I lose on the roulette wheel, so what? I'll just let a court prove it was my money anyway. I see it as a perfect plan and drift back to sleep. Perhaps I can even sell tickets.

October 4th

At 9 a.m., I wake up with that distinct realization that the very dream that seemed so sensible in the middle of the night is suddenly indistinguishable from a crazy, drug-induced hallucination. No f-ing way I was going to bet the money on a roulette wheel. I climb out of bed and begin preparing to return the money.

Sitting at my desk, I write out two checks that I need to give the bank: one for the $175 necessary to close my negative balance account, and another for $65 because I have chosen to also also return the interest that I'd accrued on the $95,000. I don't want any of the money.

I am also alerted by a call from Lisa to turn on my television. The verdict on O. J. Simpson is coming down any minute now, much earlier than anyone anticipated.

Quickly I am glued to my TV for two hours. I think they will find him guilty. I'm pretty sure about it. He's guilty. He's surely guilty. He looks guilty. He acted guilty. He's guilty. The drama of it all is actually physically exhausting to me. The verdict comes down. I can't believe it. I hoist myself off of the couch and gather my "fecal matters," headed for my safe deposit box.

I arrive at First Interstate's downtown branch. Before signing the agreement, I want to see for myself if First Interstate has left my check in my safe deposit box. Several e-mailers had guessed the bank had long ago confiscated my cashier's check.

I walk into my bank. It is more awe-inspiring and beautiful than I had remembered. I had recalled the ivory columns, gold trim, and marble floors, but I had forgotten the panoramic oil paintings of old clipper ships. Classy. And expensive. No lack of money here.

A smiling woman behind the counter asks how she can help me.

"I'd like to access my safe deposit box."

"Sure," she said, her green eyes twinkling. "What is your name?"

"Patrick Combs."

Her expression falls dramatically. Like someone just told her they'd kidnapped her kid.

"I'm sorry. What's your name?"

"Patrick Combs."

"C-o-m-b-s?" she clarifies.

I nod.

"Just a minute," she said spinning away from me and fast walking toward a woman on the other side of the bank.

The second woman takes a quick look at me and picks up the phone. I wait and am nervous. Then, exactly three minutes later, according to the clock on the wall, two men in dark blue suits with almost-black ties come purposefully through the bank's glass doors, headed straight toward me. They have no necks, but wires descend from their ears into their collars. One is talking into his sleeve. They are almost hard to tell apart, except for different sunglasses. I don't realize I'm grabbing for the counter as I fear that I'm about to get my ass dragged out the door and taken somewhere I don't want to be.

A third man appears out of nowhere on my right. "Mr. Combs, we didn't expect you for another hour, but nonetheless, it is nice to meet you. I'm Paul, the branch manager here," he says with a strained smile.

"And who are these guys?" I ask pointing my eyes to the two intimidators who have parked themselves silently at each of my sides.

"They're from Risk Management."

"Excellent, I didn't know that came with Free Checking," I mumble.

The mercenaries are still as statues while the woman who had made the call is standing close, looking visibly nervous.

"So what now, guys?" I ask, trying to discern their intentions.

"We understand you want to access your security box, so let's get you in there," the branch manager replies, still holding his smiling.

The woman, the manager, and the two suits form a circle around me as we head to the vault with only the sound of shoes clacking on the polished, marble floors. In a movie they would shoot me in the vault. Tension crawls up the back of my neck.

All five of us stand inside the vault of brushed, stainless steel boxes. Even the floors and ceilings are steel. I gaze around at all the secret stashes. Who knows what they contain? Money, gold, jewels, heirlooms, and stock notes for sure; family photographs, love notes, but quite possibly also contraband like drugs, guns, and stolen company secrets. I wonder if my box holds the most money.

I look around for my box. Only one in the entire vault has two red dots covering the gold keyholes. The woman pries out the small inserts and inserts her skeleton key, then mine. She slides out the long, slim box and steps back against the wall to give me room to open it. The two men in sunglasses are positioned between me and door, making it clear that I am to open the box in the vault. I touch the lid, sure the bank manager is about to say, "You'll notice the check is no longer there. We confiscated it. You can take the matter to court if you wish, but it was within our rights." But as I open the metal box, my cashier's check is sitting exactly like I'd left it, folded in half. The guy in the e-mail was wrong. I still have $95,000. I raise it to eye level and give it a long look. So real. So pretty with its fine red- and green-lined background. I scan it for an expiration date. None. I am still rich, I think to myself, and slip the check back into the box.

"Are you going to return the check now and relinquish the box?" one of the men without necks asks with force. I am shocked to hear him speak.

"No."

"What do you mean?"

"I mean not right now."

"I'm going to sign the settlement agreement first."

The branch manager cuts in, "Bernard Meyers says you must return the check and relinquish the box *first*."

My bank has yet to be nice to me about this check. It is too easy to picture them getting the check and then refusing to sign the settlement agreement.

"Then I need to speak with Mr. Meyers personally. Please point me to a phone."

I exit the vault and use a phone in the bank, but I am still within a spitting distance from Risk Management. "Mr. Meyers, I'm being asked to close out my safe deposit box and give back the check when we haven't signed our agreement yet. Why's that?"

"You have to do that before we sign the agreement," I hear back through the phone.

"I'll close the box, Mr. Meyers, but I'll only return the check *to you*, and *after* we've signed our agreement."

There is a pause.

"Well, we don't want you leaving the bank with the check."

"Well, I'm only going to do this one way, Bernard, so you'll have to trust me."

There is a pause again.

"Okay, close out your box and bring me the check."

I return to my safe deposit box, accompanied by my small escort team, take the check, and turn over the key.

"Thank you," the branch manager says. "And now you'll be returning the check?"

The men from Risk Management are standing very close by.

"Yes, I'm headed over there now."

"Great," he replies, perhaps noticing my eyebrows raised in a way that suggested I had a need.

"Is there anything I can do for you?"

"Hopefully. First Interstate has a policy that I have always loved: a $5 service guarantee that if the bank makes a mistake, all the customer has to do to get $5 is ask. It has kept me happy on many occasions when the automatic bank machine was broken."

His eye brows give away his surprise.

"Well, at first the bank told me the $95,000 was mine to spend, but then they changed their mind, so could I get $5 for that mistake? It's a small amount, but nonetheless." It's not easy for me to say, because I know it's a smart-ass remark.

The branch manager doesn't blink an eye. "I'm sorry," he says with feigned sincerity, "we cancelled that service a year ago. You'll notice we took down the Service Guarantee sign."

My enemy has just outfenced me. Man 1, Bank 1.

"Too bad. I loved that policy, but thank you," I reply. As I pass through the heavy, brass-framed glass doors, I tell myself it was probably a smart financial move for a bank as stupid as First Interstate. Out on California Street, I am being tailed by the two men from Risk Management.

I have only two blocks to cover to get to Bernard's office. The sidewalk under my feet is slate gray with what looks like sprinkles of diamonds. I am carrying in my pocket almost a hundred thousand dollars that I'd be giving up within minutes. Maybe I would regret it. The bank wasn't going to be grateful. I'd like a little credit for holding onto the money, for negotiating its return, for coming forward nice and polite, but it wasn't likely to happen.

I turn the corner and step onto the brick plaza in front of the reddish-brown skyscraper. A man from the Associated Press, with camera equipment slung all over him, is waiting. He tells me that it's likely that no one else from the media is coming because they are all covering the O. J. Simpson verdict.

We enter the building together, and the two men talking into their sleeves remain outside. The photographer and I are headed for the twenty-fifth floor. We don't make it to the elevator. A lobby guard, rugged in the face and uniformed in a maroon blazer, stops us. "You cannot go up with a photographer, unless you have permission."

"I'll call Mr. Meyers," I say to the photographer. "But I don't think he's going to go for it."

I use a pay phone. "Bernard, I'm downstairs with the check. I've got an excellent publicity opportunity. How about a picture of us making friends? There's a photographer from the Associated Press here with me. He wants to take a photo of me giving you the check. Is it okay with you, Bernard?"

Bernard gives a polite no. "Thank you for thinking of us, Patrick, but we'll decline."

"The photographer said to tell you it'll look bad for the bank if the photo is just of me with a caption that says, 'First Interstate Denies Any Photos.' "

"Well, he's welcome to take all the pictures he wants outside of the building, but he has to stay outside."

The photographer suggests we take some photographs on the plaza. He poses me in front of a large First Interstate logo adorning a polished marble wall. He crouches to snap, as I stand smiling. From my right, the thin and wiry lobby guard comes yelling with his walking-talkie raised like weapon. "Hey! Get out! You do not have permission to take pictures here!" He leaps into the camera's line of fire, and the photographer went into rapid fire shooting mode. I hold my pose and keep smiling. This will be a very funny photo. The lobby guard lunges toward the photographer who leaps backwards just in time to avoid a swipe from the walkie-talkie. "You can't hit me, man! You can't touch me! I'm on public property!"

The guard calls for backup. The photographer keeps shooting until I wave him to stop, and then tell him I'll have to go upstairs without him. He says he has the photos he needs and leaves.

I strain my neck up. The skyscraper looms large and unkind. I imagine executives occupying the top floors who won't show an ounce of gratitude for what I was about to do.

I enter the building nervous. As I look toward the elevator, again the maroon-suited man gets in my face.

"You can't go up. They don't want you up there," this G.I. Joe-looking man says.

"They clearly want me up there," I reply.

"You're not allowed up," he says, right before giving his back and having a whispered conversation into his walkie-talkie. Turning back to me a moment later, he says, "Own Persons, from First Interstate Security, is coming down to speak with you."

In a moment of fear, I blurt out, "I cannot and will not see Owen Persons!" Without hesitation, I spin and dash to the lobby phone booth again while yelling directly and sternly back to the lobby guard who is trying to follow me, "Don't you dare tell Owen Persons where I am. I will not see him!" My heart is pounding.

I dial Mr. Meyers and blurt out my anxiety. He cuts in quickly, "I'll come right down, Patrick, and escort you up personally."

I wait by the elevator door. The two lobby guards have a close eye on me.

I see the elevator descending, and then I hear the chime that signals the opening of the door. A very large man, dressed in black slacks and a T-shirt, is standing inside, alone. By large I mean muscular. It is not Mr. Meyers, that's for sure. I fear it is Owen Persons.

"Patrick, I'll take you up," he says, holding the elevator door and nodding for me to enter.

I do not move an inch.

"I was told Mr. Meyers was coming down. Who are you?" I ask.

"I'm Tom. Mr. Meyers asked that I escort you up. He was busy."

I ride with him up to Meyers' office and we talk about the weather.

The familiarity of Bernard Meyers' face actually feels reassuring. We sit down again at a conference room table to settle our FICAL matter. Without much ado, he produces the agreement and we both sign it. Then, I give him the $95,093.35 cashier's check. He says a quiet thank you.

"Thank you," I return.

It is all but over. After four and a half months.

"Did you bring the check to close out your account?"

"Yes, and a check to return the interest earned while it was in my account for a month."

Mr. Meyers' eyes dart to examine the sincerity of mine.

"Thank you," he says again.

He takes the checks from my extended hand. As he examines them, I hold my breath and watch Bernard lean into and examine the checks closely. His eyes squint and his head begins shaking side to side. "Patrick, Patrick, Patrick...This is a problem...This is a problem...What are we going to do here?"

This morning, I wrote the words "non-negotiable" on each.

My lungs release their air as my cheeks fight off a large smile. "Don't worry, Mr. Meyers. The words 'non-negotiable' on the face of a check don't invalidate it. It's still a perfectly legal instrument. That's my point."

"You are a piece of work," he mutters, looking at me as if he has a headache coming on. I hand him a copy of the law that backs my assertion.

"I hope you brought your checkbook, because law or no law, if the bank were to reject these checks, it would really be a problem. A *big* problem," he says.

"I'll gladly cross out the words and initial the change. Just a friendly reminder that junk-mail solicitors are your real problem."

"I'm looking into it. Now please cross 'non-negotiable' out with three lines," he says, as his face readjusts with relief.

Our settlement is done. But I hold out one last hope.

"Bernard, I have one last hope."

"What's that?"

"I *really* hoped that First Interstate would give me $5 since it made the mistake of telling me the money was mine to spend. It's such a tiny amount to ask for in light of how much I just gave back. Do you think there's any way you could help me get my $5?"

The right side of Bernard's face cracks into a small grin. He holds his gaze on me, as if thinking about his options. Then he reaches for his wallet and produces a $5 bill.

"Here. I'd say you earned it based on tenacity alone."

Bernard's compliment and gesture thrill me and remind me about my last planned step. I reach into my bag and produce two copies of my book, *Major in Success*. "They're for your daughters in college. My way of saying thank you for helping me resolve this matter. I signed them."

Bernard's pleasant smile slipped back to something disingenuous. "You are very thoughtful Patrick. It's a most gracious offer, but I must decline. Thank you, though. I have seen your book and although I haven't read it all, it does look very good."

We rise from the table and walk to the elevator lobby. Bernard then says, "Patrick, I have to excuse myself to the restroom. I trust you can see yourself out?"

"Actually, I'll join you. I have to go also." I say. Although ever so slight, I see Bernard grimace for a micro-second before replying, "This way then."

Then, just like that we are side by side at the urinals, two guys taking a leak together. "Where do you daughters go to college Bernard?"

"I'd rather not say, Patrick."

"Oh, it's just that I speak a lot at colleges and I wondered if I'd spoken where they go."

"I know you do."

"Really? Oh. Well, I'm sincere about my offer of my books, Bernard. In any case, I bet you're really proud of them both." I'm finishing up with a little shake, as is Bernard.

"I am. I must decline on the books, but I'll just say that I hope they have half as much of your tenacity." *He did not just say that!* I begin to turn to look to see if he looks as sincere as he sounded. But urinal etiquette quickly stops me. Instead, I zip up my pants. And we wash our hands in silence and exit together and walk to the elevator. "Patrick, I hope you won't encourage other people to deposit junk checks. It could get a lot of people in trouble. You didn't spend the money. Other people might not be so smart. Plus, it's problematic for banks."

"I won't. I assure you," I say sincerely. "Thank you again." The elevator announces its arrival with the sound of a chime. Its doors then separate me from the last contact I will have with a First Interstate employee.

I rotate through the revolving doors and step out onto the brick plaza. Nobody is there waiting to interview me, to ask me how I feel. I would have told them I feel good, light on my feet, and victorious for having in hand a letter people said I couldn't get. I would have kept to myself that I also felt disconcerted. Had I just won a battle of wills, but given away the prize? I had no ribbon, no cash award, no merit badge, nothing tangible to show for my victory. Nor did I receive any praise for having done the right thing. I feel inside the pocket of my jean jacket, where, only minutes before, a check for $95,000 rested. But now there was nothing there but a $5 bill and a clean conscience. A good feeling, yes, but I'd need a little time to fully appreciate it. Doing the right thing is a subtle feeling.

I proceed to walk along the busy San Francisco sidewalk wondering if this was how people felt after descending from a successful ascent up a mountain, perhaps Everest. I felt triumphant to have accomplished my peak, but a little lost, needing some time to adjust to the flat-lands. I felt accomplished, but worn down. I carried in my chest a great feeling of attainment, but I carried on me only a small letter in hand that would go straight into a box in the garage, a dead letter unable to stir any further emotion. It was a little bewildering that the greatest adventure of my life was all put away now, reduced to legal papers and black and white. Nonetheless, the last six months was my ascent up Everest, because now I knew why climbers risk their lives. They do it for the aliveness. That was the greatest gift of my ordeal with the check. It wasn't a clean conscience. It wasn't the media attention or the thrills. It was the aliveness and it was transformation of my world that smacked down from the minute that $95,000 landed into my account. From that second forward something quite unexpected happened to me. Suddenly I was alive - *really alive* - with all my senses working overtime. My mind went on super-drive. My thoughts broke their bonds. My capabilities smashed through their limitations. I dare say, I was capable of things I wouldn't have been capable of before. But most unexpected of all, it came quickly to seem as if the Universe was conspiring to help me succeed through the situation with synchronicity, unexpected help, and good luck. All because a great purpose, an extraordinary project, landed in my life. Perhaps not great or even worthwhile by other's standards, but one so remarkably engaging to me that it elevated my life to levels that I can only describe as magical. The feeling of really being alive and the magic for six months, that was the reward.

And now it was over. It's good to get both feet back onto safe ground, but out on the sidewalk, still in the shadow of the skyscraper, I can feel within me a letdown, not for the loss of money, but for the loss of great purpose. And then a makeshift, handwritten sign snaps me back to reality.

A cardboard sign in the hands of a man sitting against the wall with his bull dog says, *"My dog wants a sex change. Please help."* It makes me laugh.

"Good one! Hey, may the pup's dream come true," I say, pulling out the $5 and handing it down.

"Thanks a lot, buddy," the man says smiling.

"My pleasure," I return as I continue on my way. "Zero problem."

POST-AUDIT

The next morning, the Associated Press ran an article about me returning the check. A message was on my machine before I got out of bed. It was from a morning radio station in Baltimore that had previously had me on to celebrate that I'd cashed the check. I clicked play on my answering machine. The DJ voice said, "Patrick, you're such a disappointment. How could you give back the money? You were our hero." The lack of approval seemed like it echoed in my apartment. There were no other messages on the machine. And none to come. Aside from the AP newspaper story, this was the only opinion I would get from the media on my return of the money. I'd clearly not done what the media machine wanted. I clicked to replay the DJ's lone message. "Patrick, you're such a disappointment. How could you give the money back?" And standing there, hearing it again, I was finally certain that I'd done the right thing by returning the money. I knew because I didn't care that this DJ didn't like what I'd chosen to do, and I didn't care that he wanted me to keep the money. But more so, in that moment, I also knew that had I kept the money and faced a message on my machine that said, "Patrick, you're such a disappointment. How could you have kept the money?" I would have been crushed. I would have been criticized either way, but only one way would have bothered me. So I made the right choice.

Remember the anonymous phone call I received claiming my check was holding up a major bank merger? It turns out that in fact it was, for public relations sake. A week later, First Interstate was bought out by Wells Fargo. That same month, the banking trade journal *Institutional Investor* ran an article with the headline, "Tip to Wells Fargo: Offer a phony $10 billion check." First Interstate Bankcorp, after a fifteen-year run, was basically gone overnight. A few branches in Montana negotiated the rights to retain the name First Interstate Bank, and this new bank has since expanded to many banks throughout Montana, Wyoming, and South Dakota but has no affiliation, other than name and brand, to the First Interstate Bank I loved.

As for the people I encountered during the story, over the years, I've heard a little about a few of them.

Scott, my friend and shit-stirrer through the story, still lives in San Francisco. Last I heard he was teaching at the Art Institute. We don't speak much, for no reason, really, other than he moved to Los Angeles for a while and I moved to San Diego. But we're friends on Facebook.

My brother Mike lives in a town about a half-hour outside of Boston now. Mike became a millionaire during the Internet boom, but only for a short while and only on paper. He never got to fondle his millions. He's a wonderful family guy, very active in local politics. We're close. He was listening to morning radio a few years ago when he heard two DJs talking about the guy who, in the midnineties, had cashed a junk-mail check for $9 million and gotten away with it. Urban legend has a nice way of making everything bigger.

My mother moved to live near to my brother. The whole thing left her trusting banks even less, so she now keeps her money under her mattress.

Mitch Klass, the guy who sent the junk-mail check, was sued by the U.S. Post Office for his junk mail. He lost. On March 13, 2001, the U.S. Court of Appeals ordered much of his money be given to the Post Office. No appeal possible. But he still operates his company.

Owen Persons, First Interstate's security officer, has proved to be untraceable. For years I wondered if "Owen Persons" was just a pseudonym to signal that an "owing person" was calling? But then I met a former First Interstate executive who confirmed his name and said he was ex-military—she thought a former Navy Seal, but wasn't sure on that. Even stranger though, the very same executive who confirmed his existence had also one claim to fame within First Interstate: she was the exec who had thought up the $5 Perfect Service Guarantee. She had a clear memory of the merger being held up by some "pub-lic relations mess over a bad check."

Henry Bailey, the author of *Brady on Bank Checks*, didn't stay retired. He kept an office at Willamette Law School and continued to write legal tomes up until he passed away at age ninety, in 2006. Hats off to you, Mr. Bailey.

Bernard Meyers, First Interstate's senior legal coun-sel, became mayor and a judge after the bank folded. When I reached him for follow-up, ten years later, he was unable to say anything except, "Sorry, I can't tell you that." He couldn't even tell me if it was okay to use his real name. So I did.

And finally, Wally, the bank insider who signed his memo "Viva La Revolucion!" Until the eleventh hour of publishing this book, he had proved untraceable, because he would only sign "Wally," a nickname. I could only guess him to be somewhere in Central America leading some kind of revolt. But then in a last minute shocker, I found I had his original e-mail, and that it contained his actual name, a fact I had forever overlooked. His real name is Chris Ellinger, and when updating me on his whatabouts since the incident, he wrote me, "I abso-fucking-lutely hated working for that bank and got fired soon after that for a simple accounting error. I think they might have been on to what I did." According to his MySpace profile, he enjoys: "being a smart ass, boobs, making out, licking, leg humping, records, loud rock and roll." Aside from his brilliant sense of humor, Chris is married and owns a hair salon in Portland, Oregon, with his wife. Again, according to his profile, he would like to meet "a monkey who wears checkered pants and smokes a cigar."

As for me, immediately after returning the check, I was invited to join the cast of the crappy show *Hard Copy*, and I did a summer of "man on the street," undercover investigations for it, segments with titles such as, "Crooked Carwash?" "Does the Car Make the Man?" and "Helpful People?" It was fun and it turned into a few more appearances on the spinoff reality show *Real TV*. I also did one more major media appearance regarding the check on the *Phil Donahue Show*. Phil was fantastic. The nicest and most professional of all the television personalities I had sat down with. Truly a class act. I was sorry to see him lose his show a few years later for political reasons. In 1997, I moved to San Diego with my new wife, and today we've got two kids and two banks. I've continued the inspirational speaking ever since, accomplishing more than 1,000 speaking engagements for universities, associations and companies. The book I wrote for college students, *Major In Success,* which was published during this fiasco, is still in print after 15 years, is in two languages, and became a bona fide bestseller.

The e-mails about my online story (the genesis of this book) continued to pour in by the bucketload per day for years until I finally removed my e-mail address from the Web page. They were always amusing, primarily enthusiastic, sometimes hateful, occasionally confessional, and for a year even somewhat lucrative. Seven years after posting the story, I added a way to "Tip the Writer." Suddenly I was on the receiving end of tips ranging between $1 and $50, to the tune of several hundred dollars in my account per month for about a year. It was very fun money. And the tips weren't always monetary. "Thanks for the great story Patrick!! Here's a tip: Put a brick in your toilet where the plunger is. You'll save on water and lower your water bills." Another one said, "Store your razor in rubbing alcohol. You'll never have to buy the replacement blades again, because it's rust not use that wears out the blades—something Gillette doesn't want you to know." I've benefitted from that tip for years now. He was exactly right.

A lot of people were more than happy to thank me for my free online story, but by no means all. Some people weren't happy about my little suggestion to tip. Especially CactusRuss.

From: "CactusRuss@worldnet.att.net

Date: Mon, 17 May 2004 17:35:47 -0400

To: pcombs@goodthink.com

Subject: Patrick Combs

The silly story about the silly little man who tried to cash a fake check was slightly amusing, but I can't begin to fathom the audacity this foolish "author" has to put a pay pal link in his story and beg for tips. Too bad the bank didn't do what they should have, that is really play hard ball with him and have his hippie bum ass thrown in jail. Then the utter annoyance of a freaking pay pal link in some stupid story wouldn't spoil this entire meaningless website. I can't believe someone alludes to the fact that banks are greedy uncaring institutions would stoop to such childish levels. You want a tip? Here's a tip for ya Pat... walk blindfolded into oncoming heavy traffic, you piece of human excrement.

Sincerely,

Russell

Russell was a little late in the game of trying to make me bleed. A spirited attempt, albeit, but I'd just received way too many hate mails since first publishing the story to give Russell's any emotional impact. It also came in on a slow day, so I responded. It prompted an unexpected back and forth.

From: pcombs@goodthink.com

To: CactusRuss@worldnet.att.net

Sent: Tuesday, May 18, 2004 1:18 PM

Dear Cactus Russ, Yours was a note I enjoyed. The last line was the best—very funny especially framed as a "tip."

Best wishes,

Patrick Combs

True to any good volley, Russell responded, and what he chose to say, I never saw coming:

From: CactusRuss@worldnet.att.net

Subject: Re:

Date: May 18, 2004 5:11:40 PM PDT

To: pcombs@goodthink.com

Dear Patrick,

I was in a rather odd mood yesterday as I read and responded to your story. I normally don't send mail like that unless I know the person and are sure they are aware that it is to be taken tongue in cheek, and seeing as you don't know me, there's no way for you to know that's how I meant the message. Anyway, great story, and should I ever find myself out of the financial rut I currently reside in maybe I will send you a tip, in monetary form this time. I really did enjoy the piece, it was very well written and kept me entertained for well over an hour. I just wish I had a story that great to tell, and the talent to tell it in such a captivating way.

Sincerely,

Russell

What a difference getting back on your meds makes! The sheer volume and creativity of the e-mails that I've received over the years about this story have been one of the escapade's greatest joys.

In the years following my return of the check, I took stabs at writing and publishing this book. In its rough form online, the story was immensely popular, logging literally millions of hits and a wild stream of traffic for years and years. I don't know its numerical place as a popular Internet pass-around, but I know it was cresting near the top during its reigning years, and I know that there are entirely too many people out there who were surfing the Internet between 1995 and 2000 who stared at a screen reading the true account two hours longer than they imagined they could read a story online. On the basis of its popularity and my enthusiasm for the story in book form, I did a multitude of rewrites over many years before publishing it.

And now, there is only this left to tell. As I complete this epilogue, it's been fifteen years since I made the deposit. For the last seven years, in addition to my inspirational speaking, I've toured theaters telling the story as a one man show, titled "Man 1, Bank 0." When I started telling the story publicly, similar to when I deposited the check, I didn't expect much to happen. But the show really took off. My first performance of the "show" was in a small college classroom in the summer of 2002 for a half-dozen students. By the summer of 2005, I was selling out off-Broadway in New York. It's been a remarkable journey that has taken me to four different countries, three hundred different theaters, HBO's Comedy Arts Festival, the Just For Laughs Festival, and a whole lot of fun, but that's another story for another day. Though I will share the following brief moment.

Midway through year four of touring the show, while performing my twelfth and final sold-out show for an audience at the Edmonton Fringe in Canada, my earnings from touring finally surpassed $100,000. I'd been waiting for years to earn more than $95,000 by telling the story. To celebrate the occasion, I rained hundreds of real dollar bills onto my Edmonton audience and rolled out a huge cake with seven large numeric candles: 95,093.35. And there was a good-sport banker in the house that night who kindly agreed to cut and serve the cake.

And last, but certainly not least, in January of 2009, a dream came true. I was finally invited to perform "Man 1, Bank 0." for a room full of bankers. And they didn't like it—they loved it!

PS—My asking price for banking conferences = $9,593.35.

Viva La Revolucion!

FREE TOASTERS

I owe so many people a free toaster for helping me during this journey. Most of all, I would like to thank the funny folks at First Interstate. Without you—and you know who you are—this may have only been a free toaster in my life. I also owe a great debt to Mr. Mitch Klass. I don't know you, but I'm grateful you sent me the check. Apparently you took me off your mailing list. Why so? In any case, if you're still sending out those real checks, I'd love to be back on your list. I'd also like to thank Wells Fargo Bank. Thank you for putting First Interstate out of its misery.

Scott Leberecht, thanks for being my wingman throughout this whole dicey experience. Many laughs, buddy. Mom, thank you for being you; encouraging, wise, and unforgettable in the darkest hour of the challenge. Mike, thank you for being my best advisor on how to get the letter. Scott Edelstein, thanks for giving me courage and smarts when I needed it. Scott Wolfman, thanks for being funny when I was overwhelmed. Lisa Marlow, thanks for being there — in so many ways.

Henry Bailey, RIP. You helped me more than you'll ever know with your legal opinion and fire-brand certainty. Justin Hall, "Wally," Sharon Massey, Gary Basmajian, I so very much appreciate your help in getting the word out while it was going on. And to whomever owns Bored. com, thank you for a million hits.

My greatest thanks go to everyone who e-mailed me support while I was going through it, and to everyone who e-mailed me a good word about my story in the years after. Your e-mails were the most creative, entertaining, endlessly fascinating, and supportive part of this whole unforgettable experience.

For those of you who e-mailed me negative opinions about my choices and actions, thank you for the entertainment and counter thoughts. I like to think that ultimately you cared enough to try and help me. And for those who e-mailed to say in one way or another that I was a tool, piss off. Kidding. No, really, piss off.

Rick Broadhead, thank you for believing in this book so much despite one-hundred-plus rejections. Your belief in the book as a best-seller gave me enormous fuel for rewrites. Lyne Inada, bless you for all the publishing help. Donna King Miller, thanks for the last minute edits.

And last but not least, I'd like to thank my family: my wife, Deanna, and kids, Alyssa and Will. At the time this all went down, I'd yet to have any of you in my life, but I could have used you! You, dears, are my world.

More Ways to Live the Revolution!

Connect with Patrick.
www.PatrickCombs.com
www.Man1Bank0.com
www.facebook.com/patricklive

See Patrick's smash hit, one man theater show, "Man 1, Bank 0".
Order the DVD and check for tour dates at a theater near you at www.man1bank0.com

Have Patrick speak or entertain at your next event.
www.patrickcombs.com, email customerservice@ goodthink.com, or call (858) 759-6994.

Order additional copies of this book for friends, revolutionaries, and bankers.
If you'd like me to make a larger profit, order them through my personal site, www.man1book.com. I make an additional $3 per book when you do. If you'd rather Amazon.com have the $3, I still appreciate the order and please, if you would, post your review of the book there. For bulk discounts, (Law schools, Business schools, Ethics courses, and of course Banks), please contact customerservice@goodthink.com

Also available on Kindle and as an Audiobook.

Made in the USA
San Bernardino, CA
12 May 2016